D1195849

PERFECT
CREDIT

PERFECT CREDIT

7 Steps
to a
Great Credit Rating

Lynnette Khalfani-Cox

ADVANTAGE WORLD PRESS
Published by Advantage World Press
P.O. Box 1307
Mountainside, NJ 07092
www.TheMoneyCoach.net

Book and Cover Design:
AMV Publishing Services
P.O. Box 661 Princeton NJ 08542
Tels: 888-3396546 (toll free) 732-6476721 Fax: 609-7164770

ISBN (10-Digit): 1-932450-99-8
ISBN (13-Digit): 978-1932450996
Cataloging in Publication Data available

Printed in the United States of America
First Edition: 2010

SPECIAL SALES
Advantage World Press books are available at special bulk purchase discounts to use for sales promotions, premiums, or educational purposes. Special editions, including e-books, booklets, personalized covers, excerpts of existing books, and corporate imprints, can be created in large quantities for special needs. For more information, write to Advantage World Press, Special Markets, P.O. Box 1307, Mountainside, NJ 07092, Fax (866) 494-2461 or e-mail: info@themoneycoach.net..

TABLE OF CONTENTS

ACKNOWLEDGMENTS

I owe a debt of gratitude to a number of individuals and institutions that have helped me learn the importance of achieving and maintaining a great credit rating. First, a word of thanks to Hyundai Motor Credit Corporation, which more than 20 years ago repossessed my very first car. It was a golden brown 1987 Hyundai Excel that I drove while I was a college student attending the University of California, Irvine. At the time I thought that repossession was so very unfair, especially considering that I'd *only* missed two (or was it three?) payments. In hindsight, though, I realize that Hyundai was preparing me to become more financially responsible and credit-worthy. So thank you, Hyundai, for that traumatic experience that I've never forgotten. I've become wiser because of it.

Thanks also to all the bill collectors that have ever called me. A hearty "shout out" goes to "Mr. Johnson," a debt collector who actually called me just a few months ago from National Action Financial Services. I haven't had a debt collector call me in at least 15 years, but here was "Mr. Johnson" asking me to pay an alleged overdue credit-card bill—also from more than 20 years ago. He claimed that the account was opened in 1988 and closed in 1989. You can read in Chapter 10 about how I quickly dispatched of poor "Mr. Johnson." But just know that the sheer pleasure I took in reading this man the riot act, and the empowering feeling I got in knowing and asserting my legal rights, pretty much made up for all the other nasty bill collectors I once had to deal with.

Last but not least, many thanks to my family. I love you all, especially those relatives who have been so very understanding when I've had to say, "No, I'm sorry. I can't," when they asked me to co-sign for loans or do other things that might jeopardize my credit rating. At this point in my life I've come too far and had too many credit battles to give up my Perfect Credit rating. Here's hoping you feel that way one day too.

Lynnette Khalfani-Cox,
The Money Coach®
December 31, 2009

Other books by Lynnette Khalfani-Cox

Zero Debt: The Ultimate Guide to Financial Freedom

Zero Debt for College Grads: From Student Loans to Financial Freedom

Your First Home: The Smart Way to Get It and Keep It

Investing Success: How to Conquer 30 Costly Mistakes & Multiply Your Wealth

The Money Coach's Guide to Your First Million: 7 Smart Habits to Building the Wealth of Your Dreams

The Millionaire Kids Club Book 1: Garage Sale Riches

The Millionaire Kids Club Book 2: Putting the 'Do' in Donate

The Millionaire Kids Club Book 3: Home Sweet Home

The Millionaire Kids Club Book 4: Penny Power

INTRODUCTION

I have a bold statement to make: It's possible to have Perfect Credit even if you've been a less than perfect person. Let me repeat that another way: *You can have an outstanding credit rating no matter what your past history.* And I'm not just talking to those of you who have experienced a slip-up here or there, such as paying your Visa card late once or twice. I'm talking also to those of you who feel as though you've made a complete mess of things. It doesn't matter whether you made previous mistakes out of ignorance (such as getting a ton of credit cards when you entered college), whether you knowingly did fiscally foolish things (such as co-signing a loan for an irresponsible relative when common sense told you he would default), or even whether your emotions drove you to make long-range financial blunders (such as buying things for a former flame). You too can have an excellent credit rating.

To some the idea of having Perfect Credit might sound like a pipe dream, especially if you've been through your share of drama. Maybe you divorced an ex-spouse who was totally reckless, ran up all the bills, and dragged down your credit in the process. Or perhaps your mantra has been, "Look good now and worry about paying later." Well, "later" has come. And now those excessive shopping sprees, along with that stack of overdue credit-card statements stuffed in your drawer, mean the bill collectors have your number on speed-dial. And they aren't shy about calling either—at all hours of the day and night. Every single day.

Perfect Credit in an Imperfect World

If your credit is downright awful, you might be thinking: "I'd settle for just having decent or 'good' credit. But *perfect* credit? Yeah, right!" But, believe me; I picked this title *Perfect Credit* for a reason. The book really could have been called *Perfect Credit in an Imperfect World* because—let's be honest—we're all imperfect people, and we're certainly living in less than perfect economic times. Foreclosures abound. Credit-card delinquencies are up. Gas, food, and healthcare costs are all skyrocketing. Throw in a personal setback such as getting divorced, laid off from a job, or sick to the point where you can't work, and it's easy to see why the average person might have a blemish or two (or more!) marring her credit file. But just because you've made mistakes doesn't mean your credit is shot for life. For better or worse, you are judged in many ways by your credit. But let's not forget that even Jesus himself admonished us not to judge too harshly those who have been less than perfect (i.e., all of us) when he said, "Let he who is without sin cast the first stone" (John 8:7).

Why Everyone Should Strive for Perfect Credit

Which takes me back to striving for perfection when it comes to your credit. If you have negative marks in your credit history, I don't have to tell you what a pain it is to live with bad credit. You get turned down for credit cards and loans; you pay sky-high interest rates when you do get approved; or you have to go (hat in hand) asking family or friends to co-sign for you or loan you money. The list of indignities you suffer with poor credit goes on and on.

Lately, amid the ongoing credit crunch, even people with "good" credit histories and respectable credit scores are having a tough time. Banks have imposed new fees, raised interest rates, slashed credit lines, and even closed accounts of customers with so-called good credit. Which is why, even if you have a fair-to-good credit rating, you need to learn how to achieve Perfect Credit.

Do you plan on doing any of the following things in the next two months to two years?

⇨ Buying a house or renting an apartment
⇨ Refinancing a mortgage or getting a home equity loan/line of credit
⇨ Purchasing a car
⇨ Getting a student loan
⇨ Applying for a new credit card/switching credit cards
⇨ Co-signing a loan for someone else
⇨ Seeking a small business loan

⇨ Obtaining a new job or seeking a promotion in your current job

If so, please realize that all of these goals have one thing in common: They all require you to have great credit! So if you, or someone you know, have an immediate or near-term need for credit or a loan, you'll greatly improve your odds of getting approval, and the best rates and terms, if you follow the advice I outline in this book.

Perfect Credit is also a must-read for people who want to

⇨ **Establish credit**
* high school and college students
* recent divorcees
* widows
* elderly citizens
* immigrants
* minorities
* anyone who mainly uses cash

⇨ **Fix problematic credit**
* late payments
* charge-offs or judgments
* foreclosures or repossessions
* bankruptcies
* past-due bills

⇨ **Improve their credit**
* those with "average" credit
* consumers with "good" credit who want an A+ rating

⇨ **Maintain outstanding credit**
* anyone with superb credit who wants to hang on to that first-rate status

Perfect Credit is the definitive guide to getting and keeping outstanding credit. Think of this book as a roadmap for anyone hoping to establish perfect credit, make improvements to have stellar credit, or simply maintain a fantastic credit standing. Right now roughly 220 million

Americans have credit files maintained by the "Big Three" bureaus: Equifax, Experian, and TransUnion. Another 50 million adults in the U.S. have no credit files, either because they've never used traditional forms of credit or because their files are "too thin" to generate a score. *Perfect Credit* offers all these consumers an easy-to-follow blueprint for getting superb credit and avoiding unscrupulous firms that promise to erase bad credit.

Speaking of bad credit, about 1 out of 5 Americans has very poor credit, or "deep sub-prime scores," according to Experian. Research by the same bureau found that, between the third quarter of 2006 and the second quarter of 2009, the number of people with really low credit scores rose more than 16% to 40 million. Meanwhile the number of people with top-notch credit scores, so-called "super-prime" consumers, fell in 2009 primarily due to late payments from these once highly credit-worthy individuals. One way in which banks have responded to credit delinquencies and other challenging business conditions is by dramatically curtailing access to credit. A September 2009 report from Experian found that in the preceding 12 months banks cut credit-card lines by 17% to $3.1 trillion. And more cuts are expected. Oppenheimer & Co. analyst Meredith Whitney has predicted that by the end of 2010 lenders will slash available credit to just $2.3 trillion—less than half of the $5 trillion that was available on credit cards in 2008.

Is Perfect Credit Just About Having a High FICO® Score?

If you have never seen your credit reports, or been told your credit scores, you may have only a rough idea of your standing. If so, that's a big mistake. I don't want you to have hazy or vague knowledge about such a very important topic. I want you to be crystal-clear about your credit rating and know what specific actions you can take to maximize and even profit from it.

Toward that end it's important to explain the most commonly used credit scores. FICO® is an abbreviation that stands for Fair Isaac Corporation. Fair Isaac is a publicly traded, Minneapolis-based company that creates credit scores for tens of millions of Americans. While there are other credit scores out there (such as VantageScore and Experian's PLUS score, which I'll tell you about later in this book), FICO® scores are the most widely used by U.S. banks, mortgage companies, credit-card issuers, and auto lenders. About 90% of the top banks in America use FICO® scores. So throughout this book, when I refer to "credit scores," I'm generally referring to FICO® scores, unless otherwise noted.

FICO® scores range from a dreadful 300 points to a pristine 850 points. The higher your scores, the more attractive you are to banks and other creditors, because your FICO® score is designed to predict the chances that you will miss a payment or default on a debt. People with low FICO® scores are riskier to banks because those individuals are statistically less likely to repay a loan than are people with high FICO® scores. That's why lenders are quicker to say "Yes" to the latter group and to offer people with top-notch credit scores better deals overall.

What Exactly is Perfect Credit?

If your FICO® credit score falls between 760 and 850 points, you rate among the top tier of all consumers and have the cornerstone for what I call Perfect Credit. Getting a great FICO® score, however, is just part of the achievement. Fair Isaac reports that, among consumers with credit scores of 760 or higher, only 1% risk defaulting on a debt. So having Perfect Credit also means being able to access a whole host of products and services—mortgages, automobiles, credit cards, business lines of credit, and personal loans—at the most favorable terms available in the marketplace. Once you snag that impressive credit score, and all the benefits it entails, does having Perfect Credit today mean you'll have Perfect Credit tomorrow? Unfortunately the answer is "no."

For every single one of us, earning and maintaining Perfect Credit is ultimately a lifelong process. Once you achieve a high credit rating, you have to work consistently, diligently, and even methodically to sustain it. If you don't, depending on how you manage your credit along the way, your scores can fluctuate greatly. You may have a 680 FICO® score this year, a 795 score the next, and a 762 score the following year—only to fall back to a 681 score three years later. Therefore, you should never look at your credit scores, or at Perfect Credit in general, as an end point. The truth of the matter is that your credit scores and, by extension, your overall credit rating are constantly changing.

Think of achieving Perfect Credit as akin to earning elite status on your favorite airline. Frequent flyers who obtain elite status get all sorts of nice perks, such as complimentary upgrades to cushy seats in the First Class cabin, priority boarding and baggage handling, freedom from pesky airline fees, and bonus miles that can be used for free travel. I currently happen to be a Platinum Elite member with Continental Airlines. Platinum Elite passengers rack up 75,000 miles or more annually. If I fly a little less or change my travel patterns, I could be downgraded to Gold Elite status (50,000 miles) or Silver Elite status (25,000 miles). In fact, if I opt to restrict my travel severely, or perhaps spread my travel among multiple carriers, it's likely that I would not earn elite status at all. I am very aware of the fact that every calendar year, starting January 1, I have to requalify for my flying status. The same principle holds true for sustaining my elite credit status. As of this writing, my top FICO® score was 788. (My husband's was 775.) Every year that I manage my credit well, I am rewarded with certain perks, such as 0% credit-card deals, offers to increase my business line of credit, and a stress-free approval process when I want to apply for a loan.

My goal in writing this book is to help you earn elite credit status too. I want you to win at the credit game by using practical, proven techniques to manage your credit and debt wisely over a lifetime. I mention debt also because the debt you take on is inextricably linked to your credit standing. Remember, the whole purpose of a credit score is to summarize your risk to a lender by predicting the likelihood that you will repay a debt. I will consider myself successful if you read this book, apply its key strategies, and wind up with the following:

⇨ FICO® credit score of 760 or higher
⇨ The qualifications to get approved for any credit you require
⇨ Detailed, up-to-date knowledge about your credit at any given time
⇨ Mastery of how to manage credit wisely on an ongoing basis
⇨ An understanding of the written and unwritten rules that govern credit
⇨ The ability to eliminate excessive debt, particularly "bad" forms of debt

That is the complete definition of Perfect Credit, which is within your reach. In fact, I have developed a virtually fool-proof system for you to get Perfect Credit in just seven manageable steps. This method for improving your credit can work for anyone, regardless of age, income, professional background, marital status, or level of financial sophistication. Trust me: Once you get Perfect Credit, you'll never want to settle for anything less. I speak from personal experience. In fact, many of you have heard me talk about getting out of debt, and improving my own credit, on ABC, CNN, Fox Business Network or daytime talk shows, where I regularly appear as a guest expert.

How to Use This Book

Throughout this book I'll share my very best financial advice about achieving an outstanding credit rating. *Perfect Credit* is divided into two parts. In the first I'll describe the current economic and credit environment and how that has impacted the way a host of financial institutions deal with you, ranging from commercial banks and insurance firms to credit-card issuers and auto-finance companies. I will also teach you the basic rules, written and unwritten, about credit that you must understand in order to survive and thrive in this economy. Part II is the meat of this book. First, I'll share my own ups and downs with credit. In ensuing chapters I then will explain my seven-step Perfect Credit system in detail. If you follow it step by step, I promise that you will get the results you desire. In addition to discovering my plan for Perfect Credit, you will learn these things:

⇨ The **exact criteria that determine your FICO® credit scores** and precisely how many points your score may decline if you make mistakes, such as maxing out a credit card or missing a loan payment

⇨ The **quickest ways to boost your FICO® scores**

⇨ **Little-known strategies of credit experts** with Perfect Credit (one is my own never-before-revealed trick to get as many free credit reports as you'd like in a year instead of just one)

⇨ **How to prevent identity theft from ruining your credit** and what to do if you are victimized

⇨ What to do **if your bank has increased your rate, cut your credit line**, or closed your account

⇨ **What to say to creditors**, and what not to say, when your bills are past due

⇨ **The written (and unwritten/unspoken) rules about credit** that you must know

⇨ **How to improve your credit rating by negotiating** with your existing creditors, debt-collection firms, and "zombie" debt collectors

Make no mistake about it: The link between debt and credit standing is huge. Many of you may have read my *New York Times* bestseller *Zero Debt*, which I wrote after eliminating $100,000 in credit-card debt over just three years. While I consider that quite an accomplishment, I can tell you that learning to master credit has taken much more time and been far more challenging.

Some of the financial advice I dispense is based upon my 15-plus years of experience as a business journalist. I was previously a *Wall Street Journal* reporter and CNBC correspondent. I put my journalistic skills to good use for this book, drawing upon the wisdom of credit experts and industry professionals such as bankruptcy attorneys, consumer-rights advocates, current and former representatives from credit agencies and credit-scoring firms, financial experts, and so forth. *Perfect Credit* is also inspired by the real-life stories of people who've used the strategies I recommend to improve their credit dramatically.

I hope you agree that Perfect Credit is a goal worth pursuing. If you're ready, just turn the page, and I'll help you get on the path to a terrific credit rating.

Part I
Understanding the New Economic and Credit Environment

Chapter 1:
Wall Street's Crisis is Now Your Credit Challenge

The economic crisis that began when sub-prime mortgages started unraveling in 2006 and 2007 became a full-scale meltdown in 2008 and continues today to have a huge impact on the overall economy. At its core the crisis was about debt or "leverage" as they call it on Wall Street. Call it what you want, the simple fact is that too many individuals and far too many institutions borrowed way more than they could afford to repay. People racked up credit-card debt. They bought expensive cars, and of course they stretched for that loftiest of goals embodied in the American dream—a home. During the height of the real-estate boom, it was common for cab drivers, teachers, and others earning $40,000 or so to take out mortgages for $400,000. As long as real-estate values kept escalating, the party continued. When the credit cards got maxed out, people simply used the equity in their homes as collateral to get cash from banks. Voila! The credit-card bills were paid once again, and consumers could go back to spending. The banks were satisfied because they were getting repaid, and the economy was humming along nicely. Everyone was happy.

But you know the old saying: "What goes up must come down." So it was with real estate. Starting around early 2007, house prices stopped rising, and people were no longer able to use their homes as piggy banks. All of a sudden, when those credit-card bills arrived, they couldn't be paid off by tapping a home-equity loan or a home-equity line of credit. The first victims were so-called "sub-prime" borrowers, those with less than perfect credit ratings. The interest on their adjustable-rate mortgages shot up, causing their monthly payments to skyrocket. Most had absolutely no savings. Moreover, millions of people began receiving pink slips as corporate America went through a wave of layoffs that continues to this day. Without a job and with no cash reserves, how can you pay your house note and other bills? Many cash-strapped homeowners went 30 days past due on their mortgages. Then those 30-day delinquencies turned into 60 or 90 days. Soon a cascade of foreclosures rumbled through the housing market.

Who Is to Blame for the Financial Crisis?

Needless to say, the consumer was not solely to blame in this whole mess. The financial community definitely played a critical role in creating the problem and allowing it to persist. Banks had been too lax in extending credit, often making the riskiest loans to borrowers with the worst credit. Banks, brokerages, and other investors also made the mistake of buying investments called mortgage-backed securities. These were essentially thousands of mortgages packaged together as one big investment. In the heyday of the real-estate boom, mortgage-backed securities were big money-makers. After all, their value was tied to the worth of rising home properties. Once the real-estate crash happened, however, these investments went belly-up. Lenders, regulators, and credit-rating agencies such as Moody's and Standard & Poor all should have been sounding the alarm bells about rising debt and credit delinquencies. Instead, they failed to envision the very real possibility that a massive wave of consumers, including those with poor and good credit, might not be able to handle their crushing level of debt. But that's precisely what happened in 2007 and 2008.

Once homeowners began defaulting on their mortgages and fewer people were paying their bills, banks started to feel the sting. The money that banks had relied upon—the money that consumers had borrowed and were supposed to be repaying—simply wasn't there. Before long the financial crisis spread from individuals to institutions. In the financial world it's common for banks to lend money to each other at low interest rates. Usually these are very short-term loans, typically getting repaid within a month's time. But by 2008 banks had become leery of lending to each other for two reasons. First, banks wanted to hoard their cash to protect themselves against future losses. Second, and more important, banks were terrified of making big loans in an uncertain environment. They feared that other banking institutions might fail to honor their debts just as consumers had. Adding to the rampant fear and worry, nobody knew exactly how many bad loans banks had made or how many investments they had in toxic sub-prime mortgage debt. So just like that the credit markets came to a grinding halt. Nobody was lending money to anybody. Period.

The Credit Crunch Reaches a Tipping Point

It was one thing for a consumer credit crunch to occur, as it did during the summer and fall of 2007 when it was terribly difficult to get a mortgage loan. But when the credit crunch spread in 2008 to banks, that was another story. That corporate credit crunch proved to be too much stress on the system. The spread of the credit crunch to the corporate market, where even banks couldn't get a loan, marked a critical tipping point of the financial crisis. In January 2008, Countrywide Financial Corp. managed to avert complete disaster by selling itself for $4 billion in stock to Bank of America. Without that deal many feared that Countrywide, which had been suffering under the weight of bad mortgage loans, would have certainly collapsed.

Wall Street Implodes

Before long, however, fallout from the credit crunch and mortgage foreclosures could not be contained. There was carnage on Wall Street as centuries-old institutions failed or got bought out, some of them seemingly overnight. In a matter of months three of America's top five investment firms went under. Bear Stearns collapsed in March 2008 and was sold to J. P. Morgan Chase for the bargain-basement price of $2 a share, a deal that valued Bear Stearns at less than $240 million. (That $2 per share price was later raised to $10, but even that was small potatoes since earlier in 2008 Bear Stearns' stock had traded at $80 a share and Bear Stearns had been worth $20 billion.) Then in September 2008 two other major events rocked Wall Street. Lehman Brothers went bankrupt after federal authorities refused to rescue the company. Soon thereafter

Bank of America purchased the once mighty brokerage house of Merrill Lynch for about $50 billion in stock, less than half what Merrill was worth in 2007.

At the peak of the crisis, when it appeared that the entire financial system was on the verge of collapsing, the U.S. government got actively involved, stepping in with massive efforts to provide stability. Banks were allowed to borrow money easily, and at cheap rates, directly from the government. The government took over mortgage companies Fannie Mae and Freddie Mac as well as insurance giant American International Group (AIG). The federal government also began to scrutinize more closely the health of banks and other financial institutions. In September 2008 this change led the federal Office of Thrift Supervision to shut down 119-year-old Washington Mutual, which had been America's largest savings and loan. Once again J. P. Morgan Chase was a shrewd buyer, snapping up WaMu's banking assets for a mere $1.9 billion. A month later Congress passed a gigantic $700 billion financial-rescue package, officially called the Emergency Economic Stabilization Act of 2008, to bail out Wall Street and to encourage banks to start making loans again. Furthermore, the U.S. Federal Reserve and other government entities launched coordinated fiscal and policy actions with governments around the globe to stop the growing financial crisis from being felt worldwide. Commenting on the government's unprecedented role in shoring up financial institutions, former Federal Reserve Chairman Alan Greenspan said in an ABC interview: "This is a once-in-a-half-century, probably once-in-a-century type of event."

Despite Greenspan's proclamation, the financial crisis raged on. In late October 2009 commercial lender CIT Group became one of the latest high-profile casualties of the credit crunch. CIT had been one of America's biggest providers of loans to small and medium-sized businesses, but the 101-year-old company was forced into Chapter 11 bankruptcy—the fifth-largest in U.S. history—after CIT's own lenders refused to extend it more credit. Unfortunately, CIT Group wasn't alone in its woes. In November 2009 another lender to small businesses, Advanta, also filed for Chapter 11 bankruptcy protection. Commenting on the company's unsuccessful efforts to survive the credit crunch, CEO Dennis Alter said, "The economic debacle over the last two years devastated Advanta's small business customers and Advanta itself."

Why Banks Face a Long Road to Recovery

As of early 2010 both the American and global economy appear to be stabilizing. Nonetheless, the U.S. banking sector continues to struggle. In 2009, 140 U.S. banks collapsed. That compares to 25 bank failures in 2008 and just 3 in 2007. The Federal Deposit Insurance Corp. maintains a "watch list" of banks with troubled finances. In the third quarter of 2009, that list indicated 552 banks, the highest level in nearly 16 years, so experts predict that half or more of those banks could fail. Even if the economy were to bounce back overnight, it would not safeguard many financial institutions. "Banking industry performance is, as always, a lagging indicator," FDIC Chairman Sheila Bair said in 2009, reminding the public that problems always take a long time to work their way through the banking system.

The FDIC, Banks, and Your Ability to Get a Loan

It is important to note the FDIC's role in keeping banks healthy and how that affects their ability to extend credit or loans to you. In 1933, under the Glass-Steagall Act, President Franklin D. Roosevelt created the FDIC to provide deposit insurance to banks. The goal was to assure the public that money put into any FDIC member bank was safe, secure, and "backed by the full faith and credit of the United States government." So since January 1, 1934, the FDIC has insured bank deposits in America. Back then FDIC coverage guaranteed deposits to the tune of $2,500, a lot of money during the Great Depression. Before then, if you had money in a bank that failed, your hard-earned savings were completely wiped out.

Fast-forward some 65 years. If you had money in a deposit account, and that bank was FDIC-insured, then your money was protected up to $100,000. In 2008, during the height of the biggest financial crisis most of us have ever experienced, the FDIC raised the limits on insured accounts to $250,000. This limit will be in place until January 1, 2014, at which time it is scheduled to revert to $100,000. The FDIC insures deposit accounts that include the following:

⇨ Checking

⇨ Savings
⇨ Negotiable order of withdrawal (also called NOW accounts, which are savings accounts that allow you to write checks on them)
⇨ Time-deposit (including Certificates of Deposit or CDs)
⇨ Negotiable instruments (such as interest checks, outstanding cashier's checks, or other items drawn on accounts of the bank)

The good news for most people is that, if you've put your money in a FDIC-insured institution, it is perfectly safe up to the indicated limits. In fact, since the FDIC's inception, not a single dime of insured deposits has ever been lost.

Banks Lend (or Not) Based in Part on Their Ability to Meet FDIC Rules

There are currently about 8,100 FDIC-insured financial institutions in America. In order for a bank to declare that it is FDIC-insured, it must meet certain financial requirements by the FDIC. Specifically, banks must maintain healthy, federally mandated "capital ratios." This refers to the amount of capital (or dollars) a bank must have set aside in reserves in order to guard against potential losses. One key capital ratio for banks is called a "risk-based capital ratio," which measures the capital a bank has (such as its common stock, preferred stock, and undistributed net income/ profits) versus the amount of its "risk-weighted" assets. These risk-weighted assets can be anything from corporate bonds and consumer loans (including mortgages, auto loans and leases, student loans, credit cards, and personal lines of credit) to government notes and cash. Corporate bonds and consumer loans all carry a risk rating of 100%, meaning they are highly risky since there's no guarantee at all that they will be repaid. In contrast, government notes and cash are deemed risk-free.

If the notion of a loan's being both an "asset" and something "risky" seems a little tricky, let me explain it briefly. A loan/credit line is called a "risk-weighted" asset because, on the one hand, it is an asset, inasmuch as it represents a promise by a borrower to repay that loan/credit line (most often with interest). At the same, a loan is also considered risk-weighted because there's always a chance that the borrower will not repay a bank as agreed.

Okay, now stay with me here. To get the highest stamp of approval from the FDIC, a bank's capital must total 10% or more of its risk-weighted assets. Put another way, for every $10 that it loans, a bank must maintain $1 in capital reserves. For example, if Bank A has $1 billion in capital, and that bank has made $10 billion in loans (or extended $10 billion in credit to its customers), then Bank A's capital ratio is 1 to 10, or 10%. But if Bank B also has $1 billion in capital, and has made $20 billion in loans (or extended $20 billion in credit to its clients), then Bank B's capital ratio is 1 to 20, or 5%. These are critical measures because the FDIC insists that member banks have a more than ample amount of capital on hand to deal with any financial scenario. Thus, the FDIC categorizes banks into five groups:

FDIC Classification of a Bank	Capital Ratio
Well Capitalized	10% or higher
Adequately Capitalized	8% or higher
Undercapitalized	Less than 8%
Significantly Undercapitalized	Less than 6%
Critically Undercapitalized	Less than 2%

As you can see, the more credit a bank extends, the more capital it must be able to show the FDIC as proof of its financial strength, especially in the event of potential losses or other unforeseen circumstances. Without a healthy amount of capital, a bank runs into trouble with federal regulators. Once the FDIC labels a bank as "Undercapitalized," it issues a warning to that institution, telling it to shore up its reserves. If the bank fails to perform, and its capital ratio falls below 6%, into "Significantly Undercapitalized" territory, the FDIC has the right to step in, change the company's management, and insist that the bank take appropriate steps to remedy its capital shortfall. If a bank's finances become so dire that its capital ratio drops to less than 2%, and it is deemed "Critically Undercapitalized," that's the point at which the FDIC declares the bank insolvent and can take over management of the institution. These banks are either run by the FDIC, as is currently the case with IndyMac, which failed in 2008, or the insolvent institutions get sold off by the FDIC to another bank.

The Long-Term Implications of the Financial Meltdown

So what does all this mean for you? If you went through the ringer during the downturn (say you lost a good-paying job or maybe even lost your home to foreclosure), you may have thought that those setbacks represented the single-biggest impact on you resulting from the financial crisis. If you believe that, however, you are sadly mistaken. Don't get me wrong: Unemployment and foreclosure are major challenges, and they can have a host of far-reaching implications. But in the scheme of things those are one-time obstacles. In truth, the single-biggest impact on you stemming from the financial crisis is that the credit environment has dramatically changed, mainly because the entire banking landscape has been forever altered. This new economic environment has the power to impact you, your family, and your financial dealings for decades to come, likely for the rest of your life. You might miss that old job or your previous home, but their loss will not impact your credit or your ability to get a loan a decade from now, let alone two or three decades into the future. The new credit environment, however, will continue to have reverberations for decades.

Considering the enormous upheaval the financial community has undergone, can you see why banks and credit-card companies have become a lot pickier about to whom they lend money? They had to. It's a matter of survival. Otherwise, making too many bad loans can mean the death of a financial institution—even a century-old bank that was once seemingly rock-solid. Look no further than the spectacular collapse of Washington Mutual in September 2008 and its takeover by Chase. WaMu was founded in 1889. For many decades it was considered a mighty financial powerhouse. But with $307 billion in assets and $188.3 billion in deposits at 2,239 branches, WaMu went under in what is to date the single largest bank failure in U.S. history. In fact, as of October 2009, if you examined the biggest American bank failures ever, you'll find that 72% of those collapses (more than 7 out of 10!) occurred in 2008 or 2009. These bank failures have cost the FDIC billions of dollars and, some say, threatened the stability of the FDIC, the very institution that is supposed to back up banks.

Is the FDIC on Shaky Financial Ground?

As of June 2009, the FDIC had about $42 billion in total resources. This includes money in its Deposit Insurance Fund plus amounts set aside in the agency's "contingent loss reserves," funds earmarked for current and future losses. While the FDIC takes pains to tell the public that the agency is in no imminent financial danger and that it will not need to be bailed out by U.S. taxpayers, the agency in November 2009 adopted a new plan requiring all insured banks to pre-pay (on December 30, 2009) their estimated quarterly risk-based assessments for the fourth quarter of 2009 and for all of 2010, 2011, and 2012.

FDIC Says Costs of Covering Failed Banks is Taking a Toll

These quarterly premiums are the fees that banks pay in order to receive FDIC deposit insurance. The FDIC asked for $45 billion worth of early payments from its member institutions because the FDIC said that it had underestimated the cost of taking over failed banks and needed immediately to replenish its available funds. In 2009, 140 banks collapsed in the U.S. However, some observers saw the FDIC request as a "gimmick" to help the banking industry because the $45 billion would be treated as an asset on banks' balance sheets (a prepaid expense, to be exact) and would not diminish banks' capital or hamper their ability to lend money.

Credit Delinquencies on the Rise

Regardless of the real reason for the FDIC move, it is clear that federal regulators and banks alike have been painfully reminded that, although loaning money can be very profitable, it can also be very risky. Just look at these statistics regarding 2009 mortgage delinquencies as well as credit-card delinquencies and charge-offs. Home-loan delinquencies surged to a record 14.4% in the third quarter of 2009, according to the Mortgage Bankers Association. That meant roughly 1 in every 7 homeowners was 30 days behind on mortgage payments or already in foreclosure. Credit-card delinquencies, which include payments that are more than 30 days late, rose to 6.7% during the second quarter of 2009. And charge-offs, which are debts that banks call "uncollectible," hit 10.6% in November

2009. These credit-card delinquency and charge-off rates were at their highest level since the Federal Reserve began tracking that data, according to CreditCards.com.

Any time you or I don't pay back a loan we borrowed from a bank or credit that we utilized from a lender, what once was listed as a "risk-weighted asset" on that bank's books is labeled as something else—something ugly and potentially fatal to banks. You hear these items described in different ways, such as "bad debts," "soured loans," and "illiquid," "toxic," or "non-performing" assets. No matter what they're called, they all represent the same thing: loans made or credit extended by a bank that never got repaid.

This lies at the heart of why banks have been slashing credit lines, rejecting loan applications, and closing credit accounts. Not only do banks fear default on repayment, but they also must constantly keep their finances in top-notch shape to comply with FDIC requirements and standards. You probably have considered yourself a good bank customer if, say, you had a credit card with a $10,000 limit or a $100,000 home-equity line of credit that you rarely, if ever, tapped. You may have thought that paying on time each month or using only a modest amount of your credit would put you in the bank's good graces. Well, I hate to be the bearer of bad news, but you've got it all wrong. From the bank's perspective whatever charges you rack up on that credit card amount to a "risk-weighted asset," an unsecured loan that may or may not get repaid. And that untapped home-equity line could be considered even worse. Not only is the bank *not making* any money off you (after all, you're not paying any interest on a credit line with a $0 balance) but you're also *costing* them money. Remember that to keep supplying you with that $100,000 equity line the bank has to keep 10% of that amount, or $10,000, as capital to make the FDIC happy. Little wonder, then, that banks in 2008 and 2009 stepped up their efforts to close dormant home-equity lines and other lines of credit, including those for personal and business use.

Between April 2008 and April 2009, 41% of small-business owners reported that their card limits were cut, according to a survey by the National Small Business Association. Meanwhile, a study by Fair Isaac, creator of the FICO® credit score, found that between October 2008 and April 2009 about 24 million U.S. card holders had their limits reduced or accounts closed, even though these consumers had no new negative information on their credit reports. In the wake of the slashed credit lines and closed accounts, 8.5 million of these consumers saw their credit scores drop.

From the bank's perspective every open credit line, every outstanding mortgage loan, and every credit-card debt owed represent a serious risk that must be managed and minimized by all means necessary. J. P. Morgan Chase CEO Jamie Dimon may have summed up the feelings of the financial community when he was quoted by the *Financial Times* in February 2009 as saying, "The worst of the economic situation is not yet behind us. It looks as if it will continue to deteriorate for most of 2009. In terms of our sector, we expect consumer loans and credit cards to continue to get worse. When we look back at industry excesses in areas such as highly leveraged lending and securitization, it is clear that some of these markets will never come back." Note Dimon's use of the word "never." Clearly he sees the financial arena as having changed permanently, and so do most consumers.

In August 2009 the market-research arm of Aegis Group polled 11,400 people in 16 countries or territories around the world. Synovate found that in the preceding 12 months more than half of the respondents had changed their attitude toward money, with 84% saying that they believed it is the responsibility of each generation to leave things better for the next generation. Based on these findings, Synovate managing director Jenny Chang said that people were making "life-altering decisions based on the current global recession." About 45% of the respondents indicated their financial priority as saving money and paying off debt. Moreover, 52% of the individuals surveyed globally agreed with the statement, "My trust in financial institutions has declined dramatically." In the U.S. consumers' mindset has shifted even more starkly. A September 2009 Citi survey, conducted by Hart Research Associates, also concluded that because of the economic downturn and credit crunch Americans have made "permanent" changes to their spending habits and saving patterns. According to the survey,

⇨ 63% of Americans said their spending and saving have been "forever changed."

⇨ 62% have cut down on credit-card purchases.

⇨ 61% said they will continue to reduce their use of credit cards.

⇨ 59% said they will continue to cut back on everyday expenses.

⇨ 34% reported that they are saving and investing more.

It is noteworthy that the Citi survey found that these adjustments were being made across the board by individuals of all income levels and ethnic groups. And unlike tough economic times in the past, when Americans promised to save more and reduce debt but kept right on using credit, consumers now are following through on their plans. In September 2009, for example, the personal savings rate in America hit 4.6%, according to the U.S. Commerce Department. That is a far cry from 2005, when the savings rate was in negative territory. Also in September 2009 consumer borrowing on credit cards declined at an annual rate of 13.3%, marking a record 12 straight months that individuals cut back on credit-card usage. Even as such usage plummets, 10% of those who are using credit cards aren't paying their bills on time. Perhaps that explains why, by October 2009, J. P. Morgan Chase's Dimon hadn't changed his tune about the banking industry's struggles. In fact, his forecast seems to have become even grimmer. Speaking to investors during a conference call, Dimon said: "We know we are going to lose a lot of money next year in cards, and it could be north of $1 billion in both the first quarter and the second quarter. And that number will probably only start coming down as you see unemployment and charge-offs come down."

Now that you understand the environment in which bankers are operating, as well as how consumers are starting to respond to it, let's turn our attention to what you have to do to optimize your credit in this new and challenging environment.

Chapter 2:
The Three Basic Rules You Must Know About Credit

When it comes to credit, you need to know two sets of rules if you want to achieve the highest possible credit rating. The first can be classified as those basic written rules that banks and creditors, credit-reporting agencies, and credit-scoring companies such as FICO® tell you explicitly. These rules are well documented in the institutions' consumer-oriented publications and can be found on their websites. In a nutshell here are the three dominant rules of the credit world:

1. There is a specific formula that governs your credit score.
2. All debt is not created equally.
3. The fine print counts too.

While virtually every adult in America has access to these three written rules, a surprising number of people have never taken the time to read them, let alone understand their implications. That's a pity because knowing these basic rules is critical to fathoming the world of credit and earning a healthy credit rating. I will explain the meaning of these written rules, and exactly how you are impacted by them, throughout this chapter.

For now, though, let's turn our attention briefly to another set of credit rules. These pertain to the "read between the lines" areas that can have a massive impact on your credit rating. Think of this second set of rules as the unspoken truths that no one in the credit industry will acknowledge outright. Lacking knowledge about this second set of rules, most people flounder. Indeed, they don't even know that these rules exist. However, savvy, well educated consumers will discover these hidden rules and recognize that they are just as important as those trumpeted in black and white to the masses.

Here are the five undeclared rules about credit that you must know:

Rule #1: You must play by *their* rules to win.
Rule #2: The playing field is more level than you may think.
Rule #3: Every transaction counts.
Rule #4: The credit industry prefers to work together—without you.
Rule #5: The rules always change.

Remember how I told you that achieving a high FICO® score alone would not give you Perfect Credit? In order to master the art of managing your credit and debt over time, it is this second set of unwritten credit rules you must know and abide by faithfully. For many people this is very hard to do, not because the rules themselves are difficult to adhere to but rather because our *feelings about the rules* get in the way. Look closely at those rules once more. They may not seem that tough, but you will do yourself an enormous favor if you simply acknowledge that these unwritten rules exist and that when dealing with credit rules you should accept the following realities:

A. It's not always fair.
B. It's not always logical.
C. It's not always easy.

They Say There's a Method to the Madness

So now let us delve into the most basic set of credit rules, the written ones that banks, creditors, and the credit-scoring industry openly admit. As mentioned earlier, the first set of rules is as follows:

1. There is a specific formula that governs your credit score.
2. All debt is not created equally.
3. The fine print counts too.

We'll start with the first written rule. Did you know that an exact formula determines your credit score? It's true. The formula is calculated by the folks at FICO®, and they've been kind enough to tell consumers all about it—or at least about some of it. Has anyone ever said to you, "There's a method to my madness"? If so, the declaration probably came after he or she did something inexplicable. Well, when it comes to credit, the FICO® scoring system has been known to drive some people mad, but the experts at FICO® assure us that there is a method to their madness. In this case the madness is the formula that drives your credit score. FICO®, like all credit-scoring companies, asserts that the formula it uses is based on mathematical algorithms, complex equations, and statistical data that can predict consumer behavior. Frankly I tend to agree. However, that doesn't mean that I buy into FICO®'s analysis wholeheartedly. I simply can't because I don't know all the factors that go into the complex equations calculated by FICO®. Just as KFC doesn't reveal its secret recipe for making great chicken, FICO® won't disclose the details of how it computes your FICO® score. So for now we have to rely upon what they do tell us. Happily, that information is enormously instructive and provides an opportunity for you to nail that magic FICO® score of 760 or higher.

There is a lot of misinformation about how your credit score is calculated. However, Fair Isaac officials have said many times that what happens is basically this: Your credit files, currently those from Equifax and TransUnion, are reviewed. Certain information, roughly 22 items, about how you've managed your credit is statistically analyzed. Ultimately, five different categories are weighted to produce your FICO® score. Here is a breakdown of the five areas that contribute to your FICO® score:

1. **Payment history:** Approximately 35% of your score is based on this category.
2. **Amounts owed:** About 30% of your score is based on this category.
3. **Length of credit history:** Roughly 15% of your score is based on this category.
4. **New credit:** Around 10% of your score is based on this category.
5. **Types of credit in use:** About 10% of your credit score is based on this category.

Taking into account this information, as well as other advice FICO®

freely disseminates on its website (http://www.myfico.com) and elsewhere, you can draw some good general conclusions about which actions can help your credit and which can hurt it. For example, to increase your credit scores:

⇨ Pay your bills on time.
⇨ Payment track record is the largest component of your FICO® score.
⇨ Even if you must make minimum payments, do it!
⇨ One late payment can drop your FICO® score by 60 to 110 points.

⇨ Maintain low credit-card balances.
⇨ Don't "max out" any cards.
⇨ Try not to use too much of your available credit limit.
⇨ Spread out debt over several cards instead of carrying big balances.

⇨ Keep your older, more established accounts open.
⇨ Longer credit history is scored favorably.
⇨ Resist the urge to close an account when you pay it off.
⇨ Closing accounts can sometimes lower your FICO® credit scores.

In addition, Fair Isaac in November 2009 revealed for the first time some specific details about how various mistakes can impact your FICO® scores. Take a look at the following chart to see how credit problems, from maxing out a credit card to entering a debt-settlement program, can impact your FICO® score.

DAMAGE POINTS: HOW MISTAKES CAN AFFECT FICO SCORES		
Credit Mistake	If your score is 680	If your score is 780
Maxed-out card	Down 10 to 30 pts.	Down 25 to 45 pts.
30-day late payment	Down 60 to 80 pts.	Down 90 to 110 pts.
Debt settlement	Down 45 to 65 pts.	Down 105 to 125 pts.
Foreclosure	Down 85 to 105 pts.	Down 140 to 160 pts.
Bankruptcy	Down 130 to 150 pts.	Down 220 to 240 pts.

Source: FICO

FICO® first revealed this information to MSN writer Liz Pulliam Weston. The company emphasized that, since each person's credit file is unique, it is difficult to stipulate an across-the-board number of points that would be lost due to credit mistakes. There are just too many variables. Nevertheless, this information is valuable as a benchmark for consumers. Knowing the general factors that go into calculating your FICO® scores, as well as the impact that credit blunders can have, can help you not to stress over things that play no role whatsoever in your credit. Despite what FICO® has publicly said about credit scores, a good number of myths and misconceptions remain surrounding this topic. Be sure to separate fact from fiction.

Fact versus Fiction about Credit Scores

FICTION: If I check my credit report often, all those "inquiries" will lower my credit score.

FACT: Your personal inquiries are called "soft" inquiries and do not impact your credit score at all. You can check your credit as much as you like with no negative impact, as long as you do it through a credit bureau or a company such as FICO® authorized to issue credit reports.

EXPLANATION: Even though you may see all kinds of inquiries in your credit file, many have no bearing on your FICO® score. For instance, your score doesn't count your own inquiries as well as those from existing creditors who are reviewing your account or lenders who are trying to offer you "pre-approved" credit.

FICTION: I pay cash for everything and don't buy on credit or use credit cards, so my credit score should be excellent.

FACT: Having no credit history or never using credit can have a negative impact on your credit score.

EXPLANATION: It helps your FICO® score to have some history of paying credit obligations on time. FICO® reports that people with no credit cards tend to be higher-risk than those who have credit cards, use them periodically, and manage their debt responsibly.

FICTION: Closing my old accounts since I'm not using them any more will improve my credit score.

FACT: Depending on your overall credit profile, you can actually hurt your credit score by closing older accounts.

EXPLANATION: Generally speaking, it works in your favor to have older accounts in your credit file because it shows that you have a longer credit history.

FICTION: The most important factor in my credit score is whether or not I am "maxed out" on my credit cards.

FACT: The biggest determinant of your credit score is how well you've paid your bills on time in the past.

EXPLANATION: Your FICO® score takes into account whether you've had late or missed payments, how far past due your bills were, how long ago the late payments occurred, and whether you have any collection items such as a repossession, foreclosure, or judgment against you.

FICTION: My age, race, gender, marital status, income, or place of residence can impact my credit score.

FACT: None of those factors are taken into consideration when your FICO® credit score is determined.

EXPLANATION: Under U.S. law it is illegal to for credit-scoring to take into account race, age, nationality, religion, sex, or marital status.

Having dispensed with these myths, let's look at the second written rule concerning your credit.

All Debt is Not Created Equally

Debt is a massive problem in America. We're up to our eyeballs in debt of all types: mortgage loans, credit cards, student loans, automobile loans. Moreover, the average mortgage balance in the U.S. is about $200,000; the typical family carries a monthly credit-card balance of $10,000; the average college graduate owes more than $20,000 in student loans; and the median car note now exceeds $27,000. Is it any wonder that Americans owe $2.5 trillion in consumer debt, excluding their mortgages? Throw in another $14 trillion in home loans, and it's clear why our collective debt won't go away any time soon.

From a credit standpoint please understand that the type of debt you're carrying matters tremendously when it comes to your overall rating. (Remember the FICO® scoring formula?). I've experienced firsthand the impact that being weighed down with debt has on one's credit. I've also heard from countless individuals all around the country whose credit scores were suffering due to their having "bad" debt.

What precisely counts as "bad" debt? Nearly 100% of the time it's credit-card debt. If the balances on your Visa, MasterCard, American Express, or Discover cards have gotten out of control, you're likely doing serious damage to your credit. But other types of debt aren't good for your credit rating either, such as a department-store card you opened to get 10% off your purchase or the retail credit account you got to buy household furniture. Don't feel bad if this scenario describes you. I've made the same mistakes.

Your FICO® score is tied strongly to the credit-card debt you have. Do you recall from earlier in this book that 35% of your FICO® score is based on the amount of debt you have? With regard to this percentage, FICO® is overwhelmingly concerned with your current credit-card debt. Let me explain why.

The credit scoring system evaluates three forms of debt in your credit files: mortgage, installment, and revolving. Mortgage debt is very straightforward. This is the house note you have on your primary residence, the home-equity loan or line or credit you may have, and the mortgage you pay if you're lucky enough to have a vacation home or investment property. In short, if you own a piece of real estate, and you have a loan for which the house is collateral, you have some form of mortgage debt. Generally speaking, this is the most highly rated form of debt in the FICO® scoring system.

Next is installment debt. This refers to one-time loans that you are paying off over time by making fixed payments at regularly scheduled intervals. For instance, assume that you received a $10,000 student loan five years ago and are now repaying it. You may be making $125 payments every month. In this case your loan balance declines every month, part of your payment reducing the principle and part repaying interest on the loan. The same scenario applies to car loans. In both cases the lender knows exactly what its risk is at any given time: the outstanding balance on your loan. But the lenders also know that your balance isn't going to rise. Thus installment loans are "good" forms of debt from a credit-scoring standpoint. They are unlikely to hurt your credit ranking as long as you pay on time.

The last debt category, however, represents a potential minefield for lenders and borrowers alike. Revolving debt, such as credit cards, is the riskiest from a lender's standpoint because the lender has far less control over this debt, and you call the shots in many ways. Assume, for example, that you have a MasterCard with a $5,000 credit limit. Your balance one month might be $1,900, but last month the balance was $1,255, and the month before that it was $1,641. As it stands, neither the lender nor FICO® has any way of knowing how much you're going to charge in any given month. They can try to predict it—and they do try, as you'll learn later—but they can't know with certainty whether you will charge $30, $300, or even $3,000 on your card in the following month.

Revolving debt isn't scored favorably in the FICO® model because no one knows how much you will pay on your credit-card balance. You might decide to make minimum payments; you might opt to pay $500 against the overall balance; or you might decide to pay off the entire balance. Whatever the case, the payment amount is pretty much up to you, provided that you meet the mandated minimum. But that's not much, since most banks and credit-card issuers require only that you pay about 4% of the outstanding balance in any given month. This means that on a card with a $1,900 balance your minimum payment would be just $76 while the bank's exposure is still $1,824. The latter is the amount of money at risk for them if you don't pay up for any reason. Moreover, if you fail to pay, that credit-card balance due is no longer a "risk-weighted asset." It swings over to the "non-performing" asset section of the bank's balance sheet. Extending credit via cards can be a high-stakes enterprise. When a bank approves your credit-card application, it basically is agreeing to let you take out a loan. Issuing that credit card can be far riskier than making a loan to someone buying a car because in the latter case the bank knows exactly how much the monthly payments will be.

Speaking of cars, one final difference between installment loans, such as auto loans, and revolving debt, like credit cards, demonstrates why the latter is deemed riskier. A car loan is a secured loan. If you don't pay what you owe, the lender can come to your house and repossess the vehicle. (And don't even think about trying to hide it around the block when your payment is past due. I tried that many years ago while I was in college, but the repo man still found my Hyundai Excel and hauled it away.) A credit card, on the other hand, is an unsecured form of debt. If you charge $800 on your Visa card for that flat-screen TV you just had to have, what is the bank going to do if you don't pay your credit-card bill? They can't come into your house and snatch that 40-inch TV off the wall. So they're mainly stuck with reporting you to the credit bureaus if your payment is 30 days or more late. Of course, your account could go into collection, or they could get a judgment against you if they felt it was worth the time and money to go those routes. The central concept you need to understand is that secured loans, whether it's on real estate or automobiles or something else, are always less risky to lenders than is unsecured debt such as credit cards. As a result, that unsecured debt on your credit report, courtesy of the cards in your wallet, will always get judged more severely in the credit-scoring world.

In summary, not all debt is created equally. Credit-card debt is the form of debt most closely watched by the credit industry because it's unsecured and largely controlled by your choice of payments. Credit cards are also more frequently used than other form of debt, thereby providing more insights into your overall financial habits.

The Fine Print Counts Too

The last written rule concerning credit that is of utmost importance is the one where you're told, in no uncertain terms, that the fine print counts too. In fact, it often counts more than the "headlines" or promised benefits of any deal you encounter. How do banks, credit-card companies, retail creditors, and others tell you that the fine print counts? It's when they make statements like these:

⇨ Terms and conditions
⇨ Certain restrictions apply.
⇨ Consult rules for further information.
⇨ Complete details listed below
⇨ Full terms, rates, fees, and other costs on back
⇨ Limitations and exclusions
⇨ Please see application for all details.
⇨ Pricing and terms
⇨ Consult disclosures for important information.
⇨

Did you note that the last item above was just an asterisk? When you see that asterisk, pay as close attention as you would if you saw "Terms and conditions" because that's exactly what it means. The asterisk indicates that there is some fine print you have to find elsewhere to learn all the details involved.

So now you've been warned: If you ever see language like the statements listed above, that's your cue to read the fine print for any product, service, or deal you're contemplating. In many cases, if you take the time to read the fine print, all sorts of red flags will pop up, telling you to slow down and fully understand what you're about to do.

All Credit-Related Offers Contain the Hook and Fine Print

Oh, if I had a dollar for every time I've heard people complain (myself included) about some aspect of their credit and debt that was tied to fine print. Here's what happens in many of these cases. We get so wowed by a marketing message or deal that before we know it we're caught up in a transaction concerning which we don't understand the fine print. Or, worse, we don't even bother to read it. Perhaps we ignore the fine print because we think that only the bold-faced marketing message counts, especially when it seems to work in our favor, such as the balance-transfer promotion for a new credit card that indicates "0% for balance transfers." After you read the fine print of this seemingly attractive offer, however, you find out that the balance-transfer fees are exorbitant or that the interest rate on standard purchases is sky-high. You know what I'm talking about, right? I'll share a few stories from my own life and some other examples to explain why you absolutely must not forget that the fine print counts. After all, the institutions you deal with aren't forgetting about the fine print. On the contrary, they're counting on it to work in their favor.

A 2-For-1 Deal Doesn't Necessarily Mean 50% Off

Here is a case in point. I mentioned already that I fly Continental Airlines regularly. Well, Continental like most air carriers has a credit-card offer that allows you to earn bonus travel miles for your air and hotel purchases as well as other expenditures. What initially caught my eye, however, was one specific perk: you could get 2-for-1 First Class/Business tickets when you fly internationally and use this Continental-branded credit card to buy the airfare. Immediately I had visions of soaring across the Atlantic Ocean and trotting off to Europe in style and comfort with my husband— all for half price. At first I thought, "Wow! That's like getting 50% off! What a great deal! All I have to do is to buy one first-class ticket (Continental calls its service BusinessFirst), and then my hubby travels free. Whoopee! What a no-brainer for travel buffs like us!" Then I settled down and decided to read the fine print.

One key detail in the fine print of that offer made the whole deal far less enticing. Yes, you could in fact get 2-for-1 BusinessFirst tickets anytime you booked international airfare using the credit card, but there was a

43

special requirement. Some might call it a "catch." However, I'll be fair to Continental and simply call it a "requirement" because the airline did exactly what it was supposed to do and disclosed the requirement right there in black and white. In the fine print, yes, but it was there nonetheless. Here's what the requirement stipulated: to get those 2-for-1 BusinessFirst tickets you must purchase a *special type* of BusinessFirst ticket, namely one *full-fare* ticket. If you've ever flown to Europe or any place else internationally and paid for a full-fare First Class/Business ticket (I, for one, have not), you know that the average cost for such a round-trip ticket can be very pricey. For instance, when my husband and I flew BusinessFirst to Stockholm, Sweden, in August 2009, we traveled in Continental's first-class cabin. However, the tickets we purchased, at a cost of about $2,000 apiece, were "discounted" BusinessFirst tickets as opposed to "full-fare" tickets. At full fare first-class tickets would have been about $8,800 each.

So much for what I thought would be a killer 2-for-1 travel deal. In reality I wouldn't be getting a "half-off" deal, as I wrongly assumed by honing in on the "2-for-1" marketing message. Most "2-for-1" offers of this type don't "save" money at all because of the high cost of that initial First Class/Business ticket. Nevertheless, due to other attractive features, I'm still considering the Continental offer. And I'm a person who weighs very carefully when and under what circumstances I apply for credit. At the very least, if I do decide to go for the offer, I'll be glad that I went into the transaction with my eyes wide open. And, again, I can't honestly fault Continental. They disclosed what I'd have to do—right there in the fine print of the credit-card offer.

The Importance of Reading the Fine Print

It's been said that "The big print giveth, and the little print taketh away." In many ways that's true. Here's why the fine print counts, often more than the bold-faced advertising or marketing message you may have seen in an offer.

⇨ The fine print is where you'll learn what you must do to qualify for something.

⇨ The fine print is where you'll find out when the benefits promised apply, when they don't, and when they can change, expire, or be revoked.

⇨ The fine print is where you will discover all the restrictions, exclusions, and other rules that govern a deal.

Therefore you must always think about any loan, credit offer, agreement, or special deal as having two parts: the hook and the fine print. The hook is designed to do just that—"hook" you into saying "Yes." The hook is the bold-faced advertisement or marketing message that grabs your attention. It will be something enticing such as "No Money Down," "Low 4.9% APR," "Only $9.95," "Cash Back Bonus," or "Free." The fine print invariably has less appealing language. It covers the nitty-gritty details of the offer, including its limitations, pricing, fees, terms, and conditions. The fine print is most often located at the end of an offer or agreement. In the case of online offers, the fine print is typically one or more click away from the hook. While the fine print may be difficult to read, hard to find, and not easy to understand, it is there nonetheless, and it's your responsibility to read it. If not, you can put your credit standing and your finances at serious risk.

The Credit Ding That Even the Money Coach Never Saw Coming

Here's another true story that shows the importance of reading the fine print. Coincidentally this story also involves a travel-related matter. In February 2009 I went to Tucson, Arizona, to serve as the keynote speaker for a YWCA personal-finance conference that was sponsored by HSBC Bank. About 500 women attended. It was a smashing success, and I met a lot of lively and interesting people. While in Tucson I rented a car from Avis to get around town and thought nothing of using my debit card to pay my rental-car bill.

A few days after I returned to my home in New Jersey, I received an email notice from FICO®. I use FICO®'s credit-monitoring service as well as the 3-in-1 service offered by FreeCreditReport.com (more later on the benefits of credit monitoring). In this case FICO®'s "Score Watch alert" was letting me know that there had been an "inquiry" on my credit report. The FICO® alert also notified me that my credit score had dropped 14 points. I was flabbergasted and suspicious. At first I thought that there must have been a mistake or that perhaps I was a victim of identity theft. I knew with 100% certainty that I had definitely not applied for credit of any form, so there should have been no "inquiry" popping up in my credit file. I immediately clicked on the information sent from FICO® and discovered that the inquiry in question came from Avis. An inquiry from Avis? That's puzzling and certainly not correct, I thought. I knew, of course, that I had rented a car from Avis, but I hadn't requested credit or applied for a job, either of which would have given Avis the right to pull my credit file.

After a few moments of mulling the situation over, I decided to contact Avis directly. When a customer-service representative got on the phone, I really let her have it. I wasn't foul-mouthed or nasty, but I was certainly indignant and voiced my dismay that Avis had had the gall to pull my credit. I told her that I was a person who tried to maintain excellent credit and that Avis had marred my credit file by causing my FICO® score to tumble 14 points. The employee listened attentively, seemed as bewildered as I was about why a credit inquiry occurred, and got somewhat apologetic. When I demanded to know what Avis was going to do about the situation, she transferred me to a supervisor, who also listened calmly as I explained my complaint. "Why in the world would Avis do a credit check on me?" I finally demanded. Then the supervisor asked me whether I had paid with a debit card. When I said "Yes," she patiently explained that actually Avis *does* have the right to pull the credit report of consumers who opt to pay with a debit card. Furthermore, she pointed out, Avis tells you this in the fine print.

At first I didn't believe her. I've rented cars for years; I thought I read my contracts carefully; and I had even just opened a corporate Avis account for my business. Moreover, in all my previous travel my credit report had never been pulled just for renting a car. "Show me where in the fine print Avis discloses this!" I practically shouted at the poor supervisor. She searched and searched, and after a few minutes she guided me to the Avis website and pointed out this passage: "In most cases U.S. locations will perform a credit check for debit-card renters to determine credit worthiness at the time of rental. The renter must meet Avis's minimum criteria in order to rent." "Oh," I replied, as I sank bank in my chair. It was as if she'd drop-kicked me. Then I gathered up my final bit of tempered outrage and added, "Well, I'm still upset about it. I think it's ridiculous for Avis to do this, and I should've been warned about it when I rented the car." Despite my righteous indignation, during the conversation I pulled up the email confirmation of my reservation that Avis had sent. Sure enough, it too disclosed that same provision buried in the fine print. Somehow I had simply missed it, probably because I thought I was scoring such a good deal when I rented my car online. Little did I know that the real score I should've been worrying about was my credit score. In my wildest dreams I never imagined that using my debit card could actually hurt my credit. On the contrary, I thought I was being more responsible by using my debit card instead of running up unnecessary debt on a credit card.

Homeowners Who Fail to Heed Fine Print Face Disaster

Okay, enough about me. Let me give one last example that may sound familiar. During the foreclosure crisis it was very common to hear homeowners lament that the home loans they received were misrepresented to them. Tales of woe abounded. Some people thought they were getting fixed-rate loans but wound up in adjustable-rate mortgages. Others decried punitive clauses that seemed to come out of nowhere, such as a hefty pre-payment penalty that made it impossible to sell or refinance or a balloon clause that meant a big lump sum was due just a year or two after getting the mortgage. There were even homeowners who got scammed into illegal transactions, such as selling a property at an inflated price to "straw buyers"—people who just wanted to deceive a bank and had no intention of ever taking possession of the homes they "bought."

I don't doubt for a minute that untold numbers of homebuyers were duped into signing on the dotted line by unscrupulous mortgage brokers and others trying to make a quick buck on a house deal. However, it would be foolhardy to suppose that all the homeowners out there with sob stories were simply the unwitting victims of con artists. A more likely scenario is that many of these homebuyers were thrilled at the prospect of buying a home, glad of approval for a mortgage, and never read the fine print of their home loans. Or if they did read them, they clearly didn't understand what they were reading and therefore should

47

have asked more questions. Unfortunately, many of these homebuyers, including well intentioned people with good values, wound up in foreclosure. They learned the hard way a lesson that I hope you can learn without experiencing it directly: You should always read the fine print and fully comprehend the terms and conditions of any agreement you make. It can have enormous implications for your credit and your overall finances.

Chapter 3:
The Five Unwritten Rules about Credit Nobody Tells You

Have you ever struggled with a difficult situation or made poor choices due to rashness, inexperience, or lack of knowledge only to have someone come along later with a nugget of information that would have helped you sail through your tough time? If so, you may have thought, "If only I knew back then what I know now, life would have been so much easier."

In many ways that's how most people learn about credit. At first they make mistakes—lots of them. Then they suffer through trial and error, doing some things right but flubbing others. Often it's not until someone in the know comes along and passes on a key piece of wisdom that you finally have an "Aha!" moment. It's at this point that everything starts to become clear. Then you know what to do to manage your credit wisely, and what not to do, to get the best outcome.

The following information is designed to teach you the unwritten rules about credit that govern your life. As previously mentioned, there are two sets of rules you need to know to achieve perfect credit. The first set, the written regulations, is just a starting point. Equally important are the unspoken and unwritten rules that pervade every aspect of credit. If you don't know these rules, or if you fail to heed them, your credit rating will never reach its pinnacle, and you'll always be frustrated by the credit-scoring system.

Here again are the five unwritten rules about credit:

1. You must play by *their* rules to win.
2. The playing field is more level than you may think.
3. Every transaction counts.
4. The credit industry prefers to work together—without you.
5. The rules always change.

Some aspects of the credit system, or the credit-scoring world, may baffle you because the rules go against all logic and at times even contradict each other. Other rules, when implemented and applied in real life, may seem patently unfair to you. And then there are rules that seem terribly difficult, if not impossible, to comply with. Let me simply caution you that it's far easier to play the credit game—and I use that term as shorthand for navigating the world of credit—when you understand the rules. So even if you don't agree with something, the system is what it is. It's far better to adopt the right mindset about these rules upfront than to feel stung by them later because you didn't know they existed or you objected to them on the basis of logic and fairness. If you can get your mind (and emotions) in check and just accept that not everything in the credit universe is fair, logical, or easy, it will be far less taxing for you to cope with this system. Having said that, let's look at each of the unwritten rules about credit.

You Must Play by *Their* Rules to Win

Of all the unspoken rules that dominate the credit universe, none is more difficult for people to swallow than this one. For starters, when someone else dictates the rules and you have no say in the matter, it seems as though the deck is automatically stacked against you. You might be saying, "Why do *they* get to set the rules?" or "Who the heck are '*they*' anyway?" In this case playing by "*their*" rules means playing by all the rules set forth by the credit industry and all its players—banks, credit-card issuers, credit-reporting agencies, credit-scoring companies, and so on.

Tens of millions of people in this country opt out of the credit system, wage a never ending battle against it, or live by their own rules, often sabotaging their credit in the process. Consider, for example, the roughly 50 million adults who operate outside the credit mainstream. They have no credit file whatsoever. Many never had a credit card, took out a mortgage, had a student loan, or paid a car note. Granted, a lot of these individuals are potential newbies to the credit world—students, widows, recent immigrants, and so on. For whatever reason they've not gotten around to applying for credit. A sizeable segment of these people, however, have consciously chosen not to participate in the credit system. Some will proudly tell you, "I've never had a credit card and never will." Others once did have credit but because of bad experiences in the past, or due to perceived or real injustices they suffered, now stay away from all things credit-related. "I don't mess around with credit cards any more. They're nothing but trouble," these people will tell you. In fact, some people go so far as to check out of the entire financial system, having no credit arrangements, no checking or savings accounts, and no dealings with any major banks or financial institutions.

Bucking the Entire Financial System

Did you know that there is an entire cottage industry within the financial-services community whose sole reason for being is to reach out to so-called "unbanked" consumers? According to estimates by the FDIC, there are approximately 28 million unbanked households in America. That's just over 25% of the nation's 110 million households. The FDIC says that the problem of being unbanked affects poor and minority communities disproportionately, with 7 out of 10 unbanked households earning less than $30,000 a year. Half of the unbanked once had bank accounts but now choose not to, instead using the high-cost services of check-cashing firms and payday lenders. The unbanked don't get traditional loans. If they need a short-term loan, they get "credit" from payday-loan outfits. I call payday loans "credit" because they are "signature loans," meaning that you sign on the dotted line, just as when you sign a credit-card agreement. With payday loans, however, you're agreeing to give the lender cash from your next paycheck in exchange for an advance today.

The Danger of Payday Loans

Payday lenders routinely charge interest rates of about 400% on an annualized basis. That's a ridiculously high price to pay for "credit"! So why do people go to a payday lender when they're short on cash, especially when they could use a credit card to pay for something or even take a cash advance? There are numerous reasons, not the least of which is a lack of basic banking services in many communities. Also, many payday-loan clients had previous credit problems or couldn't qualify for a regular credit card. Another issue is at play here too. Many of these consumers out of the credit mainstream do not have the financial skills to play by the credit-card industry's rules. One of the obvious rules is that you must repay what you owe, or at least a partial amount, by a set date. But guess what? Payday lenders don't have that rule, at least not as a hard and fast requirement. They'll let you slide by and "roll over" your payday loan. Can you guess why they have such "flexible" rules? It's because "roll over" loans impose hefty fees, making them enormously profitable for payday lenders. The average payday-loan customer who falls into the trap of such arrangements winds up paying over 1,000% in interest, according to a study by Georgetown University researchers. Unfortunately, the average person who gets a payday loan typically rolls it over, getting an average of 1 payday loan per month or 12 in a year. A payday loan is thus one super-expensive form of "credit" you should never accept.

Payday Lenders Get Creative to Evade the Law

By the way, payday lenders are getting sneakier than ever before. In the wake of tough laws clamping down on them, many payday lenders are starting to offer what they call "installment" loans. These are still essentially payday loans, but the loans are stretched out over longer periods of time in order to help payday lenders bypass various state regulations governing short-term loans. For example, in December 2005 the state of Illinois adopted the Payday Loan Reform Act (PRLA) that regulates loans of 120 days or fewer. So what did payday lenders do after that law was passed? To circumvent a host of loan restrictions and consumer protections offered by the PRLA, many Illinois payday lenders began offering look-alike "installment" loans of 121 days or more. Needless to say, the net effect of these so-called "installment" loans is the same as with traditional payday loans: the consumer ends up in an expensive, long-term cycle of debt. In fact, according to the Woodstock Institute, which conducted a comprehensive analysis of two of the largest payday lenders in Illinois, these high-cost installment loans are even more expensive for consumers than traditional payday loans.

Were You Suckered or Did You Fail to Play by Their Rules?

Another example that illustrates how people can't play by the credit industry's rules can be seen in promotional offers of all kinds. They could be a retailer's "no payment, no interest" offer or perhaps a "teaser" rate for a new credit card. The most important terms that govern these deals are usually in the fine print, but many of us rarely read those vital terms. Then we get angry when after six months all the interest on purchases we made has accumulated and is due, or the initial low rate of interest expires. You didn't get suckered. You failed to play by the rules by not paying up within the six-month period specified in the fine print.

And don't get me started talking about student loans. Way too many recent college graduates ding their credit after leaving school simply because they don't start making payments on time. In most cases you must begin repaying federal and private student loans either six or nine months following graduation. When some college grads choose to attend graduate school, they know that they are eligible to get their loans deferred, but many fail to play by the rules and don't actually *apply* for a deferment. They assume that just having "in school" status is enough. Unfortunately, it isn't. To get that deferment, you must fill out paperwork requesting it, as required by student-loan rules. Otherwise your student loans will be reported as late on your credit report.

A final case in point. You finally pay off a credit card and decide to close the account, just to make sure you're not tempted to run up the bill again or simply because you don't need the card any more. Well, the credit-scoring industry has already said, very clearly, that closing an account, especially if it's a long-standing account, can have an adverse impact on your credit rating. It all depends on a host of factors such as how long you've had other accounts open and the overall mix of credit in your file. Meanwhile you're thinking, "It doesn't make sense for me to keep a credit card that I'm not even going to use." So you close the account. There you go—defying the rules of the game and putting your credit at risk.

In many of these cases, do you know why we buck against these rules? It's because in our hearts we feel that they're not right. We're silently, on in some cases loudly, protesting something we believe isn't fair, logical, or easy. As a result, we opt not to comply, or we opt out of the credit system entirely. I said it before, and I'll say it again: The complex world of credit isn't always fair, logical, or easy. We can all agree on that. But at the current time this is the system we've got. Opt out of the credit system if you wish, but do so with full knowledge of the risks and rewards that go with playing outside the rules.

As Kenneth Lin, CEO of the website CreditKarma.com puts it, "Some people think credit is biased or inherently unfair, so they just don't use credit at all. You can do that," Lin adds, "but it just makes your life so much harder."

The Playing Field Is More Level Than You May Think

Now a bit of good news: Even though the credit industry has the upper hand, the playing field is more level than you may think. Economic, technological, social, and political changes in recent years have tilted the balance of power toward you and me. Specifically, the playing field has leveled out due to four factors: competition, regulation, advocacy, and Internet time.

How Industry Competition Works to Your Advantage

Do you routinely get credit-card offers in the mail? If so, I'm not surprised because the average U.S. household gets dozens of these offers annually. In fact, banks and other credit-card issuers send out more than five billion offers each year. That is a sign that the credit-card industry is highly competitive. Fortunately, such heavy marketplace competition is a big equalizer when you have to deal with banks and other lenders. Consider the company that issued the card you use most frequently. That company knows you are constantly being courted by other financial institutions. This fact gives you leverage in dealing with your bank, since it doesn't want to lose you as a customer—assuming, of course, that you've been paying your bills. A competitive banking environment gives you more wiggle room to negotiate with your credit-card companies, say to ask for a lower interest rate or to request waiving of an annual fee. If you're a good customer and pick up the phone to make such a request, you're likely to get a "Yes" because your credit-card company doesn't want you to take your business elsewhere.

Let me tell you a true story of something that happened to me, in the middle of the credit crunch no less. I had used a CitiBank MasterCard to make several large purchases. That combined with my using the card while in the Cayman Islands apparently threw up a red flag for Citi's fraud-protection unit, which contacted me to confirm that I had, in fact, made the transactions. When I replied that I had, a representative not only thanked me for my time but also quickly reviewed my account and told me he was *lowering* my interest rate several percentage points. How often does that happen? Needless to say, I was happily surprised and quickly expressed my thanks, but only after first confirming that there was no "catch" involved such as buying some service or applying for new credit. Nope, he said. The new and lower interest rate would become effective immediately, and it was simply Citi's way of thanking me for being an excellent customer since the year 2000. While I have been a very good customer with Citi, I also recognize savvy business practices when I see them. This was not only fine customer service. In a competitive environment it was also a shrewd move on the part of a bank that wants to hang onto valued clientele.

Regulation Reforms the Credit-Card Industry

Consumers scored a big win in 2009 when President Barack Obama signed the Credit CARD Act, which consumer advocates say will stop or prevent unfair or deceptive lending practices by banks and credit-card issuers. The law was formally called the Credit Card Accountability, Responsibility, and Disclosure Act. In August 2009 two provisions of the legislation were adopted. The first required your credit-card company to give you a 45-day advance notice before an interest rate hike, up from 15 days. During that period you have the option of rejecting a rate hike and closing the account. Under this scenario you have the right to pay off the debt over five years at your original rate of interest. However, there's one big loophole in this change to the law. The 45-day advance notice requirement applies only to credit cards with fixed interest rates. Unfortunately, more than 90% of all credit cards issued are variable-rate cards. In addition, just before the 45-day rule took effect in 2009, many issuers of fixed-rate cards started notifying customers that their cards were being converted to variable-rate cards.

Even bigger credit-card changes begin in February 2010, when a host of other rules take effect. For example, the reform law prohibits credit cards from being issued to individuals under 18 and prevents issuers from retroactively increasing your interest rate unless you've been 60 days or more late in paying your bill. Also, effective in July 2010 new rules from the Federal Reserve require banks to provide better disclosure to their credit-card customers.

Given all these changes, you may have already noticed that many credit-card companies have begun imposing various fees, raising interest rates, slashing credit lines, and canceling accounts altogether in an effort to manage risk, offset reduced profits, and generate new revenue streams. According to CreditCards.com, in mid-December 2009 the national average rate of interest for "bad credit cards" (i.e., cards issued to those with bad credit) was 13.74%, but rates can go much higher. Industry observers say the highest-rate card in 2009 came from First Premier Bank, which offered a sub-prime credit card with a whopping 79.9% interest rate. That card, marketed to people with bad credit, had just a $300 credit limit. The company's CEO, Miles Beacom, defended the unusually high interest rate by saying that it was "based on the risk associated with this market."

In response to the onslaught of new fees and other activities by banks, members of Congress considered accelerating adoption of the new credit-card laws, making them effective in December 2009 instead of February and July 2010. While that never happened, lawmakers did continue to debate a bill introduced in December 2009 to cap credit-card interest rates at 16%. Currently banks can charge whatever interest rate they like on credit cards as long as the information is fully disclosed to consumers. Therefore, First Premier's 79.9% interest rate card is perfectly legal. The company's CEO said that the bank will "allow customers to make the decision whether they want the product or not."

While the banking industry's move toward more careful risk management and closer scrutiny of credit applicants will be a long-term trend, I expect that the rise of fees and interest rates, and other punitive actions such as arbitrarily closing accounts, will be a short-term phenomenon. Only time will tell. I nevertheless predict that political forces, regulatory oversight, and industry competition will keep banks in check. For starters, the outcry of consumer opposition to objectionable bank practices is being heard more clearly now than ever before. In addition, politicians and regulators alike are under pressure to rein in unfair banking activities that unjustly enrich financial institutions at the expense of the public. Finally, sheer economic forces will come to bear. Banks will be more competitive in the long run by dropping excessive fees and unnecessarily high interest rates for good customers. And when one bank stops imposing annual fees to win over new business, the rest of the industry will take note and do the same thing. On balance, therefore, credit-card reform has created a more level playing field and will compel more fairness in credit-card lending and marketing practices.

The Growth of Consumer Advocacy

The growth of consumer advocacy has been an important ramification of the recent financial crisis. Because economic and credit problems were so widespread, there was a surge of interest in helping Americans become more financially literate. All of a sudden economic news dominated the front pages, not just the business section, of newspapers. You couldn't turn on the television without hearing some reference to money issues, no matter whether you were watching a news program, sit-com, or daytime talk show. Suddenly everyone seemed to recognize that Americans' spending-happy ways, over-reliance on credit, and mismanagement of debt were profoundly damaging to us personally and as a nation. Amid this growing recognition, consumer advocates of all different stripes emerged—from actors and politicians to consumer-watchdog groups and community-based organizations.

At the height of the mortgage crisis, activist groups such as the Neighborhood Assistance Corporation of America(NACA) vehemently protested what they described as unfair and predatory lending practices in many minority communities and beyond. Their protests, which included everything from organized demonstrations to boisterous rallies outside the homes of banking executives, have won serious concessions for financially troubled homeowners. Specifically, NACA convinced the country's four top lenders—Bank of America, Citigroup, J. P. Morgan Chase, and Wells Fargo—to lower the mortgage payments of cash-strapped borrowers. Having a lower house payment obviously frees up cash to pay one's other bills. So if homeowners using these lenders ran into financial trouble, they might be more likely to get loan modifications, a move that could stave off foreclosure and protect the borrower's credit rating. NACA is known as such a fierce consumer-advocacy group that the *Wall Street Journal* in 2009 reported that NACA "terrorizes" bankers in the fight against foreclosures. NACA officials likely take that as a compliment. After all, it was NACA founder Bruce Marks who told the *Journal*, "We have to terrorize these bankers."

Internet Time Heals All Wounds

Have you noticed the speed with which most credit-related transactions take place in today's economy? In an age when five billion pieces of information are added to credit files monthly, two million reports are ordered daily from credit bureaus, and the average person's credit report is updated five times per day, information moves far faster than ever before in history. In this age of the Internet, everything simply occurs faster. As a result, your credit rating is impacted more quickly and mostly for the better. Thanks to technology you can fill out a credit-card application online and get approved instantly. If you're house-hunting, you can apply for a mortgage using your home computer and, because the loan officer is using an automated underwriting system, get a same-day pre-qualification or pre-approval letter. If your old jalopy of a car finally gives out on you, and you need to get new wheels in a hurry, you can simply head to a local dealership, have them pull your credit file, and—presto—by day's end you can drive off the lot in a brand-new automobile. In short, thanks to the Internet, we all benefit by getting the credit we want far more quickly than was ever previously possible.

Happily, when it comes to negative aspects of your credit rating, the advantages of Internet speed still hold true. In this case the credit industry forgives your past mistakes faster than ever before. For instance, a little more than a decade ago, if you had a serious problem with your credit such as a bankruptcy or foreclosure, you were pretty much a pariah. No bank would consider you for major credit for at least five years. In some cases prospective lenders wouldn't risk extending credit until that bankruptcy fell off your credit reports altogether. Today, although credit-reporting rules remain the same concerning how long that bankruptcy can be reported in your file (ten years), what has changed is the credit industry's view of past transgressions. Banks and other lenders now routinely offer mortgages to people just two years after a bankruptcy is discharged. FHA loans allow people to get a mortgage one year after bankruptcy if the filing was caused by a hardship as opposed to fiscal mismanagement. In fact, you can still be in a Chapter 13 bankruptcy, repaying creditors over three to five years, and get an FHA loan provided that you've made your most recent 12 months of trustee payments on time, can pony up a 3.5% down payment, and prove you can afford the new mortgage.

Similar advantages accrue from the credit-scoring side of the industry. Your FICO® scores obviously take into account your payment history. Having one late payment can knock 50 to 100 points or more off your credit score. The impact of late payments, however, doesn't have to last seven years, even if the negative information stays on your credit report for that long. According to FICO® executives, their scoring model takes into account how recently the late payment occurred. In fact, the "recency of delinquency is really important in the new [FICO® scoring] model," says Tom Quinn, Vice President of Scoring at FICO®. "It's going to be super-predictive of your future payments in the near term. So more recent behavior is really heavily weighted in the credit scores."

In other words, a single late payment that happened last month will be more detrimental than one that happened 12 months ago. Similarly, if your last late payment occurred two or three years ago, it's very likely that your FICO® scores could have rebounded completely, provided you've paid all your bills on time since having that prior credit lapse. How's that for a more level playing field? Internet time. You gotta love it.

Every Transaction Counts

Hopefully I've convinced you that, for a host of reasons, the deck isn't completely stacked against you when it comes to managing your credit in this new economic environment. Having said that, you still have to understand, and abide by, the written and unwritten rules of the credit industry. And the next unwritten rule to learn is that every transaction counts. And when I say "every" transaction I mean it. Retailers, credit-reporting agencies, credit-scoring companies, and of course lenders are increasingly watching every financial transaction you make. Have you made an online purchase of shoes lately? Somebody tracked it. That's why the next time you're working at your computer, or simply surfing the Web, you'll see a pop-up advertisement featuring shoes. Ditto for school supplies, furniture, electronic gadgets, or anything else you purchase. But the scrutiny goes beyond just monitoring what you buy and then trying to sell you more of it. Retailers, lenders, and credit-scoring firms are capturing a wealth of data about your financial habits to tell them who among us is the most credit-worthy.

So what exactly are they watching? In a word, everything. They're looking to see whether you accept credit-card offers—online, in the mail, or via telephone. They're gauging whether you're likely to accept a balance-transfer offer for an initial low-interest rate, only to cancel the card when the offer expires or when a better deal comes along. They're looking at the types of stores you frequent and whether you spend money (i.e., use your credit cards) at "risky" establishments such as bars, clubs, and casinos. They're also poring over data regarding your housing, and that includes both renters and homeowners. For those of you who rent, they're looking at whether you've consistently paid your rent on time and whether you've ever been evicted. For homeowners they're looking at whether your mortgage is a fixed-rate or adjustable loan, whether you have a home-equity loan or line of credit, and, if so, how much you typically tap and how often. If it seems that the credit industry has got a spotlight trained on you, they do. But you don't have to be blinded by it if you manage your financial affairs properly.

When I say that *every* transaction counts, let me make something clear: I'm not just referring to business transactions that involve loans. Every transaction means just that. Every economic exchange you make—every credit, loan, or contract agreement you enter into, every financial move that can be documented—all of it matters greatly. Do you think that your dealings with cell-phone companies, water and energy services, and other public utilities aren't being monitored? Think again. About 100,000 organizations supply information to credit-reporting agencies. These organizations include banks, lenders, collection agencies, credit-card companies, leasing firms, and utility companies. Even libraries have been known to rat on delinquent patrons for having an overdue book!

The same holds true for various municipalities around the country. Chicago and New York City will report you to collection agencies for failing to pay parking tickets. And as cash-strapped cities try to cope with budget shortfalls and a tough economy, you don't have to be Nostradamus to predict that many more cities will soon start using collection agents to pursue "small" debts due from local citizens.

Other transactions you may regard as minor can wind up having serious ramifications for your credit rating. That unpaid $14.95 magazine subscription you ordered can come back to haunt you. Those music videos you neglected to return could land you on someone's collection list. And even that hospital co-payment or medical debt for which you've been sent a bill yet again, for the umpteenth time after your insurer refused to pay, that too could damage your credit rating.

Fortunately, there is one recent change to credit-scoring concerning small debts, which are sometimes called "nuisance" accounts. In August 2009, Fair Isaac rolled out to all three credit bureaus its newest general-purpose FICO®-score formula dubbed FICO®08. Under this new version FICO® pledges that it will disregard collection accounts and other dings on your credit file when the original balance owed was under $100. "The logic there," says FICO®'s Tom Quinn, "is that for small dollar amounts, like a collection notice from a public library system, the model will now bypass those and not consider those to be negative. Any kind of derogatory public information that's less than $100 will be excluded," Quinn adds. This certainly has the potential to help boost your FICO® score if it were impacted by such minor blemishes. However, despite FICO®'s saying that it won't include those small accounts in its scoring methodology, the debts nonetheless remain on your credit file, and some lenders may require that you resolve those issues or pay off those debts before approving you for a loan.

Transactions large and small take on greater importance amid the credit crunch because these days Big Brother seems to be peeking into your laptop, using a sky cam to watch where you go, accessing your Blackberry or iPhone, and placing wiretaps on your phones. Okay, maybe it's not that bad, but you get my point. An incredible amount of information about your finances is being captured, analyzed, and dissected in ways you probably never imagined. I predict that in the future this trend will increase.

The Credit Industry Prefers to Work Together—Without You

The fourth unwritten rule about credit is that the industry prefers to work together—without you whenever possible. I'm not saying that they have no need for you or that they don't want to have some dealings with you. After all, consumers provide valuable feedback and constitute a revenue source. And companies in the credit industry realize that, if they don't address the consumer, their competitors will. All in all, however, many folks in the credit industry would be quite happy if you just went away and not made any fuss about your credit.

Why do I say that the industry sometimes considers you a thorn in its side? First of all, you have to realize that credit-scoring firms had to be dragged into having any direct interaction with consumers. The credit industry only started giving consumers a peek at their credit scores in 2001, despite the fact that the first commercial credit scores were created by the founders of Fair Isaac more than 50 years ago in 1958. It wasn't until the 1970s, however, when credit-card usage grew tremendously, that banks began widespread use of credit scores to reduce card delinquencies. A couple decades later, in 1989, Fair Isaac released the first general-purpose credit score used to predict a consumer's overall riskiness to a lender. It was only at that point that any serious consideration was given to educating the consumer about credit scores. Until then credit-scoring firms like Fair Isaac, as well as the credit bureaus themselves, had mainly focused all their attention on lenders and businesses that needed to obtain credit information in order to manage risk. They're were playing together nicely, thank you very much, until consumers and consumer advocates started demanding to know the exact same information to which lenders were privy.

More recently, credit industry players have shown other examples of how they can work together even as they compete with one another. In 2006 the "Big Three" credit bureaus jointly developed their own credit score called the VantageScore. Doing so raised the ire of Fair Isaac, which sued and alleged anti-trust violations. That lawsuit is still pending. I frankly don't have a big problem with the credit bureaus getting together. The point of their creating a joint score was to minimize variation in people's credit scores. You see, credit scores are based on the underlying information contained in each of your credit files. Thus, if Equifax, Experian, and

TransUnion have different data about you, naturally your scores based on those three reports will vary. This is often exactly what people find. In getting together, the Big Three tried to come up with a statistical model to lessen variation among the bureaus. All in all, I don't fault their efforts but use it to point out that the bureaus, while competitors, are willing to work together. The primary point of contact they have with you as an individual comes when you order a credit report, purchase a product, or dispute a mistake in your file. In the last scenario you have to fill out a dispute-resolution form, online or in the mail. And once you dispute something, what do the credit bureaus do next? Do they come back to you and ask you to prove what you said or to verify it independently? No, they really don't. They may allow you to send in supporting documentation to bolster your claims, but essentially the bureaus go to your creditors as the ultimate arbiters of the truth. They go to the lenders, banks, collection agencies, or whatever entities reported you, and the credit bureaus say, "This individual disputes the information you provided. Do you agree or disagree?" And based on what that lender or creditor or bill collector says, their response determines what goes into your credit report. Either the information is confirmed by a creditor, and it stays on your report, or the creditor can't verify what was initially reported, and the information is dropped from your file. I have to question whether the creditors are right 100% of the time. Nevertheless, what they say goes. This is standard operating procedure. The dispute-resolution process is legal, and it's yet another example of how the entire industry works together, maximizing the flow of information among themselves and minimizing interactions with consumers.

So if you ever feel that you're not exactly receiving full disclosure about some aspect of your credit report or scores, just remember that the system was designed that way. The credit industry (not all players, but certainly many) wants to maintain control over and access to credit information for risk-management and profit motives. They don't want you to have the same insights and information that they do, nor do they want you to quash their creative maneuvering. As one blogger wryly noted about the credit industry, specifically bank creditors and credit-scoring firms, "You have to admire their resourcefulness. Step 1: Cancel credit card because you don't use it enough. Step 2: Lower your credit score because you had a credit card cancelled (or limit lowered). Step 3:

Send dozens of offers through the mail for new credit cards with higher rates and fees. Repeat as often as needed."

Again, in fairness to the credit industry, I don't want to paint all the players with one broad brush. Clearly some exceptions to the rule exist. Indeed, a select number of companies are bolstering their efforts to provide credit education for consumers, as opposed to just selling the public loan products, credit reports, credit scores, and credit-related services. Overall, though, I believe that the industry can do a much better job of communicating with consumers, advocating financial literacy, and giving the public more insight into the complex world of credit management and scoring.

The Rules Always Change

After you master the written and unwritten rules concerning credit, you may be tempted to rest on your laurels a bit and think, "Now I finally get it," but I caution you to remain vigilant about the credit universe because invariably the rules will change. In fact, the rules always change. The formulas for credit scores get tweaked. As previously mentioned, Fair Isaac in 2009 made dramatic changes to its FICO® scoring model, dubbing it FICO®08. Banks also change their policies. Lenders get more or less strict; credit-card interest rates go up or down. And laws and regulations governing the entire credit industry come and go, or get amended, all the time. The landmark Fair Credit Reporting Act, initially adopted in 1971, has been amended numerous times, including changes starting in 2005 that, thanks to the FACT Act, for the first time required each of the three national credit bureaus to provide consumers in all states with a free copy of their credit reports. You can get them online at http://www.annualcreditport.com. Indeed, with credit the one thing you can count on is change. So just because you know something credit-related to be a fact today doesn't mean that it can't be totally upended tomorrow.

Part II
How to Have Perfect Credit
(Even If You've Been Less Than Perfect)

Chapter 4:
My Ups and Downs with Credit

A ny time a financial institution, credit-card company, bank, or other entity puts a negative mark on your credit file, what they're really doing is bad-mouthing you to the rest of the world. They're telling anyone who cares to listen that you were 30 days (or more) late in paying a bill, and they're damaging your reputation in the process. After all, when you have late payments or serious blemishes on your credit report such as a charge-off, judgment, repossession, or foreclosure, you've essentially been branded as a financial deadbeat. Like many people you may have gotten into financial trouble through no fault of your own in the wake of a job layoff. Or maybe you fell behind on your debts due to extenuating circumstances such as an illness that resulted in medical bills your insurance company wouldn't cover. Nevertheless, a bad credit history puts a host of people and institutions on notice that you're not to be trusted. Poor credit implies that you can't (or won't) honor your obligations, that your word is not your bond, and that from a financial point of view you're a bad risk. You wind up with the economic equivalent of a scarlet letter simply because you didn't pay your bills on time.

It can be hard to restore a reputation once it's damaged. This is obviously the case in the financial world, where one mistake can mar your credit file for seven or ten years. The same general principle applies in other realms too. Look at what happens to politicians involved in ethics scandals, businessmen accused of corruption, or celebrities busted for extramarital affairs. I'm not judging these individuals. We've all done things that we would never want to see broadcast on the news or put on the front page of a newspaper. I'm pointing out, though, that recovering from a blow to your reputation is tough, and sometimes that one negative situation becomes the thing for which you are remembered. Don't let that happen to your credit. Blemishes in your credit file can plague your reputation for what feels like an eternity, hampering your ability to get ahead. Having spectacular credit makes life so much easier, and being burdened with lousy credit can be one of the most stressful things you'll ever face. I know because I've experienced both extremes.

Sign on the Dotted Line

At one point in my mid-30s, I considered renting a townhouse. When I visited it for the first time, a friendly manager at the housing complex raved about the property's many amenities, highlighted its prestigious location, and assured me that the school district ranked among the best in the state. After I decided I wanted the place, the good-natured manager suddenly turned all business. She briskly reviewed my written application, asked me for a security deposit, and then told me point-blank: "If your credit is good, no problem. You'll get approved. If your credit is bad, you won't." Clearly she had done this many times before. I smiled, looked her in the eye, and replied with confidence: "My credit is perfect. I'm sure I'll be moving in soon." With that she immediately went online to get my credit report. In less than three minutes she examined nearly every financial detail about me for the past dozen years: mortgages I had paid off, cars I owned, my credit-card balances, and, of course, my payment history for all these things. When she was satisfied that not a single blemish was to be found, she pulled herself away from her computer terminal, swiveled around in her black leather chair, and said pleasantly: "You have very excellent credit. When would you like to sign the lease?" It was a done deal.

Red Carpet Treatment

Weeks later, as I began furnishing my new residence, I paid for certain household goods upfront. However, with two big-ticket furniture purchases, I opted to take advantage of zero-percent financing deals. In the first store the sales clerk ran my credit. Then he quickly told me that I qualified for the best terms available. At the second retail establishment a saleswoman asked me whether I was sure I wanted to apply for credit. "Citi Financial is very strict. You have to have really good credit, or they reject you," she warned me. I suppose she wanted to spare me the embarrassment of being declined if my credit wasn't stellar. I told her to proceed, and two minutes later I was approved. "Is there anything else you'd like to buy," the saleswoman now asked, "because you have a line of credit up to $7,500." "No, thank you," I replied. In both of these instances I received the proverbial "red carpet" treatment based entirely on the strength of my credit standing. Here's why: My credit-card debt was minimal, I had a 760 FICO® score, and my triple-A credit report would make even Donald Trump green with envy. But it wasn't always this way.

The Bad Credit Blues

I used to have terrible credit, not just "bad" credit. I'm talking truly horrible credit. Multiple late payments, charge-offs, court judgments for non-payment, and even an automobile repossession marred my credit file. While I never had the granddaddy of poor credit, a bankruptcy, I nevertheless had the kind of credit file that must have made bank officers sit around and laugh out loud. I can just picture them reviewing my credit-card application. We'll call them Joe and Harold.

Joe: "Hey, Harry, you gotta get a load of this one! Can you believe she even applied? What was she thinking—or should I say, what was she smoking—to even hope she would get approved? Maybe instead of our form rejection letter, we can write her and say: 'Due to your pitiful payment history, young lady, you aren't getting a credit card, a loan, or anything else for years to come!' Ha, ha, ha!"

Well, okay, maybe that's a stretch. Perhaps the many credit-card rejection letters I received just got spit out by some computer, and no one gloated over my sorry state of affairs. But I have to figure that at my worst, when my credit score was no doubt in the low 500s, I was unquestionably a classic case of "How to Ruin Your Credit in No Time Flat."

Easy Credit Courtesy of Your College Campus

Like many of you, I got my first credit card as a college freshman. In fact, the day I moved into my on-campus apartment at the University of California, Irvine, I walked into the modest room I shared with my roommate and saw that credit-card applications had been placed on the beds. No sheets, no blankets—just "special invitations" courtesy of MasterCard, VISA, and American Express. "Wow! I must really be an adult now," I figured. "I can get a credit card in my own name." I soon discovered that credit-card offers were rampant on campus. They were posted in the student center, stapled on message boards, thumb-tacked or taped onto poles, and piled high on tables anywhere students hung out. Of course, any wall that had those handy brochure holders affixed to them—and there always seemed to be tons of them right outside large lecture halls—was sure to be plastered with solicitations from any number of banks and financial institutions. That was roughly 20 years ago. If you walk the halls of most college campuses today, you'll see that not much has changed, though the Credit CARD Act has made it somewhat tougher to target the college crowd.

Financially Illiterate College Student + Too Much Credit = Financial Disaster

Some of the credit-card marketing I encountered as a student was subtle, but most of it was in-your-face and no-holds-barred. "Want a free T-shirt?" asked solicitors as I strolled from one class to another. "Sure, why not?" I thought. Like most 18-year-old college kids, my mind was somehow automatically programmed to gravitate toward four-letter words such as FREE. "Great. Just fill out this credit-card application," they urged. When I went to buy textbooks at the book store, what happened there? Along with my books and receipts, the cashiers stuffed more credit-card offers into my plastic shopping bags. While all this credit was being thrown at me, nobody told me how to manage it responsibly. Forget the fact that I didn't even have a job. Nobody advised me that just because I "qualified" for a $5,000 credit line didn't mean that I should accept it. Nobody cautioned me to make my payments every month without fail, or the defaults would haunt me for seven years. Nobody taught me that making minimum payments on credit cards with 20% interest rates basically meant that I'd be in debt for life. So I guess it's no surprise that by the time I was 21 years old I owed nearly $10,000 to a slew of creditors. Making matters worse, the first car I'd ever purchased, a new Hyundai Excel, wound up being hauled off by the repo man despite my efforts to hide it blocks away.

The Road to Recovery

Luckily, after earning my bachelor's degree, I got a job, negotiated fiercely with bill collectors, and started paying off the many debts I'd accumulated in college. From that point on I became diligent about always paying my bills on time. I never again wanted to deal with irate debt collectors and their annoying phone calls at all hours of the day and night. Even having learned my lesson about "No late payments ever" and after earning my Master of Arts degree, I still wasn't schooled about the proper use of credit and how to manage debt wisely. In fact, as time went on, I used credit more and more—almost as if it were cash. I actually thought that I was being "responsible" as a credit user just because I was making minimum payments each month without fail. Little did I know that I was fooling myself, and allowing myself to be seduced, by the lure of easy credit. Unfortunately, "Buy now, pay later" became my financial motto.

Debt-Free at Last

By the time I was in my early 30s, I was swimming in debt—$100,000 worth of credit-card debt, to be exact. Fortunately, I managed to pay it all off in three years without resorting to bankruptcy. In 2004, when I paid off the last of my massive credit-card debt, I finally began to enjoy the benefits of having zero debt and outstanding credit. Topping the list of benefits is peace of mind. I never have to sweat over my credit card's possibly being rejected when I'm enjoying dinner out with friends, paying for a hotel room, or buying any kinds of goods and services. Nor do I fret over whether I'll be approved for anything. Banks now fall over themselves competing for my business.

The Pleasures of Perfect Credit

I'm guessing that given the chance you'll also want perfect credit and the pleasure of a smooth, hassle-free process when you're ready to acquire a gold credit card, finance a new car, or buy a home. When you're applying for a loan and have perfect credit, it's like playing Monopoly and having a "Get out of jail free" card up your sleeve with every roll. You can't lose. But having perfect credit affords you more than just the best rates and terms on loans. It also means that you'll pay less for life and auto insurance. Moreover, people with outstanding credit get promotions and new job offers far more readily than do people with poor credit histories. Did you know that under the law your existing employer, or a prospective employer, can check your credit and use that information for making a promotion or hiring decision about you? Compared to a person with bad credit, the individual with stellar credit saves a remarkable amount of money and earns a heck of a lot more too.

The Story of Bill and Skip

Here's a tale about two 40-year old guys who are best friends. We'll call them Bill and Skip. From the time they were teenagers both Bill and Skip dreamed of becoming successful corporate sales executives and enjoying the finer things in life—you know, nice house, sporty cars, designer suits, the whole works. Bill and Skip attended the same college, and both graduated with business degrees and a 3.5 grade-point average. They married around the same time, and each now has two kids of the same ages, 7 and 5. Since Bill and Skip are sports buffs, neither one smokes; in fact, the two of them are in great shape because they work out together every weekend at the local gym. Although Bill and Skip both work for the same Fortune 500 company, that's where the similarities end.

You see, Bill always pays his bills on time. He's made it a point in his life to handle his financial affairs responsibly. So he keeps his debts at manageable levels, always keeps up with his obligations, and safeguards his credit in every way he can. In fact, he makes payments on his $400,000 mortgage ten days ahead of the due date. Skip, on the other hand, plays fast and loose with his finances. He skips Visa payments every now and then, sometimes just because he's too busy to get stamps from the post office. Because he's on the road so much, Skip often forgets to mail his cell-phone payment when it's due. "What's the big deal if I pay it a couple days late?" Skip thinks. "They're still going to get their money." In addition, Skip has missed making his mortgage payment on time twice in the last year, once when he was on vacation and another time when he was traveling for a business conference. The same thing happened with his car payment for the Lexus he drives. Unfortunately, Skip didn't have automatic payments set up online to make those payments in his absence. "I can't be bothered with that. Those things are too complicated, and besides I'm too busy," he said when his wife suggested putting their bills on automatic payment plans to avoid those constant late fees. Skip's wife was tired of arguing with him about their money problems, so she just let it go. But when it came time for Bill and Skip to get loans and insurance, the wayward Skip was shocked at how much he had to pay. When the two friends compared notes, here's what they found:

⇨ Mortgages—Although Bill and Skip both took out 30-year, fixed-rate mortgages for $400,000, Bill's monthly payment is $2,300 a month while Skip's is $2,800. Compared to Skip's, Bill's mortgage payments are $6,000 less per year, saving Bill $180,000 over the life of his loan.

⇨ Auto Loans—Both made equal down payments to finance their late-model Lexus automobiles, but Bill's payment is $400 a month while Skip pays $550. By the time the cars are paid off in five years, Bill will have doled out $9,000 less than Skip. And since the average American family buys seven new cars in a lifetime, that $9,000 gets multiplied seven-fold for a total lifetime savings of $63,000.

⇨ Credit Cards—Bill and Skip are carrying $3,000 balances on their Visa credit cards. However, since Bill has perfect credit, his interest rate is just 8.9%; Skip's is at the default rate of 28.99%. So Bill pays around $27 in monthly interest while Skip is hit with charges of $87 each month. In five years' time Bill saves $3,600 in interest costs. At this rate, over the next 30 years, Bill will pay $108,000 less in finance charges.

⇨ Life Insurance—Both men bought $500,000 whole-life insurance policies. Bill's costs him $320 a month or $3,840 yearly; Skip's costs $410 a month or $4,920 annually. Over the course of 40 years, Bill will save $43,200 by paying $153,600 for insurance compared to $196,800 spent by Skip.

⇨ Auto Insurance—Though both own cars of an identical year, make, and model, Bill's insurance costs $1,800 a year while Skip's runs $2,340. Bill's five-year savings on auto insurance is $2,700 ($9,000 paid by Bill versus $11,700 paid by Skip). Over 35 years Bill's savings add up to $18,900.

A Promotion Won and Then Lost

All told, Bill saves at least $413,000 because of his lifetime of perfect credit. That's nearly a half million dollars that Bill keeps in his bank account, simply for paying his bills on time and managing his credit wisely. But the financial benefits don't end there.

Bill and Skip are also up for promotion to Senior Vice President of Sales. Even though they're competing for the same position, they're still buddies. Bill tossed his hat into the ring for promotion not knowing that Skip was going to go for it. When Bill found out that Skip was interested in the job, Bill thought about withdrawing his name. "The truth of the matter is that you are the better salesman," Bill told Skip, adding that "Everyone knows you're a shoe-in for the promotion because of your outstanding sales record. You deserve a promotion." As it turns out, the boss saw it that way too. After interviewing four candidates for the job, the boss picked Skip. But because the job paid $100,000 annually, the human resources department performed its customary background check, running Skip's credit report in the process. Within 24 hours Skip's promotion had been rescinded. The high-paying job ultimately went to Bill, who received a $25,000 raise. Neither guy thought it was fair, but as Skip's boss said upon withdrawing the promotion, "Hey, it's nothing personal. It's just business."

Apparently the company figured that bad credit meant that Skip wouldn't be as trustworthy and might be tempted to steal customer funds if his own money problems worsened. Skip went home seething mad.

He consulted a lawyer to see whether his boss could legally offer him a job and then take it back because of Skip's bad credit. The attorney advised Skip that unfortunately what the employer had done was perfectly legal. When Bill went home, he was ecstatic. He did the math and realized that over the next 25 years the extra $25,000 in salary meant he would generate $625,000 in additional income before retirement, not including any other raises. As you can see, paying his bills as agreed allowed Bill to save and earn a total of $1,038,100 more than poor Skip, who continued to skip payments and wound up constantly penalized for his lousy credit.

Good Credit Isn't Good Enough

Some of you might be asking, "Why do I need perfect credit? Isn't 'good' credit good enough?" The answer, simply put, is "No." If you've got horrendous credit, then by all means upgrading to good credit would be a major improvement. But why stop there? The difference between having good and having perfect credit is like the difference between a high-school student's getting 1,200 on his SAT exam versus scoring a 1,500 or a perfect 1,600 on that all-important exam. Is 1,200 good enough score to get him into many schools? Sure it is. But wouldn't it be awesome if that same student aced the SAT and pulled off a 1,600 or a near-perfect score? What do you think his college prospects would be then? I'm sure he'd have virtually every university admissions office in the country vying to recruit him, offering college tours, and extending generous financial-aid packages—in short, doing everything in their power to attract that top-tier student.

Sometimes it's nice to be sought after like that. And consumers who have A-1 credit are the most sought after on the planet. I don't care if you're in Dallas, Texas, or Durban, South Africa. When you manage your credit wisely, you're in the driver's seat. Are you ready to get perfect credit? In the pages that follow I'll give you the keys—figuratively speaking, of course—to your very own dream car. And trust me, when you've got spectacular credit, the ride is superb. After all, when you're traveling first class, getting there is half the fun.

Seven Steps to Perfect Credit

What would you say if I told you there is a way you can systematically develop perfect credit? Would it be worth it to you if I gave you a regimen you could follow, seven fool-proof steps to build your credit, just as professional athletes follow a fitness regimen to develop perfect abs or a perfect jump shot? Well, the truth of the matter is that you can develop perfect credit if you stick to a game plan. Once again, that's where I come in. As your Money Coach I'll give you all the pointers you need to strengthen your credit standing and avoid the aggravation faced by those who have bad credit. And what's best of all is that everything I'm going to reveal is totally feasible, practical, tried-and-true wisdom that works. So let's begin boosting your credit reputation in order to strengthen your financial muscle. It's about time you started training to get not just good credit but perfect credit!

Here's what you need to do to follow my unique PERFECT CREDIT SEVEN-STEP SYSTEM:

P—Pull your credit reports and credit scores.
E—Examine your files and enroll in credit monitoring.
R—Reduce debt and manage bills wisely.
F—Fix errors and protect your credit.
E—Enhance your credit file constantly.
C—Contact creditors and negotiate.
T—Take time to educate yourself.

Let me walk you through each step in the following seven chapters.

Chapter 5:
Pull Your Credit Reports and Credit Scores

When did you last check your credit reports? Was it a few months ago, a few years ago, or something in between? And what about your credit scores? Have you ever gotten a firsthand peek at them? If you want to acquire top-notch credit, the first step is (a) to pull each of your credit files from the three major credit-reporting agencies—Equifax, Experian and TransUnion; and (b) to get your credit scores, which are marketed by various companies and calculated based on the information contained in your credit reports.

A shocking number of people have never seen their credit files or received their credit scores. Such ignorance is costing them gobs of money. A survey by Washington Mutual and the Consumer Federation of America concluded that being in the dark about credit, and about how the credit-scoring system works, is costing individuals in America as much as $28 billion a year.

Without pulling your credit reports and credit scores, you can't give yourself a proper financial checkup—let alone improve your credit rating. It's no different than the person who says, "I've never been to the doctor" or "I've only been to the doctor once in the past five years." Would you treat something so important, your physical health, so callously? Likely not. Then please don't be so callous as to disregard something that's also of high importance—your financial health.

To become a better steward of your overall finances, you absolutely must pull your credit reports and check your credit scores, including your FICO® scores and others that can give you firsthand information about your credit profile. There are no ifs, ands, or buts about it.

Thankfully, under a law called the FACT Act, you have the right to get your credit reports free of charge once every 12 months from Equifax, Experian, and TransUnion. The credit bureaus have made it easy for consumers by streamlining the process of reaching all three bureaus simultaneously. The credit bureaus jointly operate a website (www.annualcreditreport.com), use the same toll-free number (877-322-8228), and have a common mailing address to which you can write in order to get your free annual report. That address is Annual Credit Report Request Service, Post Office Box 105281, Atlanta, GA 30348-5281. (I've provided the individual addresses, phone numbers, and websites for each credit bureau at the end of this book.) In addition to your credit reports you should also get your FICO® credit scores, and other scores too, though in most cases you have to pay for them.

In this chapter let's look first at what it takes to pull your credit reports, where you can get them, and some tips on making it as easy as possible. We'll also look at the process of obtaining your credit scores, including your FICO® credit scores.

Federal Law Entitles You to Free Credit Reports

Federal law mandates that the credit bureaus provide all adults with a complimentary credit report once every 12 months, but only if you ask. Again, the credit bureaus provide these reports online at www.annualcreditreport.com. So this should be the starting point for anyone who wants to review his or her credit history.

Once you take the time to request that free credit file, what can you expect? For starters, you'll be asked to give identifying information about yourself: your full name, date of birth, Social Security number, and so on. To safeguard your privacy, the credit bureaus will also ask you a detailed question about some area of your personal finances that presumably only you know. For instance, their security-verification question might be the following type of multiple-choice inquiry:

Three years ago, you took out a mortgage loan from which lender?
A. Wells Fargo
B. Citibank

C. Bank of America
D. J. P. Morgan Chase
E. I did not receive a mortgage from any of these lenders.

After your identity is verified, you will be routed to each credit agency. All told, it should take you less than 15 minutes to retrieve all three credit reports maintained by Equifax, Experian, and TransUnion online at www.annualcreditreport.com.

Why You Should Get Your Three Credit Reports Simultaneously

Once you're all set to request your credit files from the bureaus, you have the option of getting those reports in one of two ways: all at once or over a period of several months, perhaps even up to a year. Some experts recommend that you get a single credit report at a time, staggering them every four months, so that you see your credit files throughout the year. Under this scenario you might retrieve your Equifax report in January, get your Experian report in May, and then secure your TransUnion report in September. The following year you would repeat the cycle in January, May, and September. Advocates of this method suggest that, to execute this strategy, you should set up email notifications, text alerts, or other calendar reminders to help you keep tabs on when to request a credit file throughout the year.

Although this process can work, I strongly suggest a different method. I think you'll be far better off getting all three credit reports at once and signing up for a worthwhile credit-monitoring service. I'll discuss credit monitoring at length in the following chapter, but for now let me just say that the good ones are extremely valuable, credit-enhancing tools that that not only will pay huge dividends in your quest for Perfect Credit but also will take the hassle out of trying to remember to stay on top of your credit.

So why it is most advantageous to get all your credit reports simultaneously, as opposed to getting those files in a staggered fashion over the course of many months? It boils down to four primary benefits.

1. Speedier Resolution of Errors
If something is wrong in any one of your credit files, you want to know

about it and get it corrected pronto. When you pull all three of your credit reports, you're able to tell whether any or all of your files have inaccuracies about your credit history. If so, you can begin to dispute those mistakes immediately. If you waited to get your credit reports, months could go by with damaging, erroneous information on your credit files without your knowing it. And don't forget that, if you're seeking any loans, mistakes in your credit files could cause your application to be rejected or force you to pay higher interest rates than you should.

2. Clarity About Differences and Discrepancies in Your Credit Files

By looking at all three credit reports together, you will gain insight into a host of potential differences and discrepancies contained in your various files. For instance, does one of your reports show that student loan you paid off, but the other two lack that information? If so, you'll want to have that positive payment history (i.e., a record of your successful loan payoff) added to those two other credit files. And what about other discrepancies? Are you listed as an authorized user for a certain credit-card account on your TransUnion report but only as a co-signer for that same account on your Equifax file? The difference may seem subtle, but it can impact your credit rating. Lastly, have you ever pulled your credit scores and not understood why the Experian score came in at 700 while the Equifax rating was 675 and the TransUnion score just 658? These discrepancies can frequently be explained by disparities in your credit files such as inquiries listed, amount of debts shown, or the payment track record reported in each of your files.

3. Better Credit Education

Perhaps the chief benefit of viewing all your credit reports together is the amazing amount of financial education you will get about your credit profile just by looking at the highlights of each file and the way that similar information is presented differently in each report. Every one of us learns differently, and you'll find that you understand some aspect of your credit better (or not as well) from the reports generated by Equifax, Experian, and TransUnion.

My Experience in Examining My TransUnion, Equifax, and Experian Reports

For example, after pulling my most recent TransUnion report, my first response was to squint because I didn't like the way the information was presented. The tiny print in the file was hard to read, and there were images that at first glance confused me. Furthermore, all my accounts were listed alphabetically, making it difficult to determine which accounts were closed versus which ones were open. It reminded me of an engineering report with little boxes and things I had to decipher. All in all, the presentation of information by TransUnion wasn't initially attractive to me.

In contrast to the TransUnion credit report, I liked the visual layout of my Equifax and Experian reports. My Experian file was easy to read, presented in a summary format, and clued me in to salient points such as the number of open and closed accounts in my file and the fact that all my accounts were in good standing with no delinquencies. My Equifax report was also nicely presented. I appreciated that Equifax had done a lot of analysis for me. It too told me the number of open accounts I had; gave me balances, available credit, and credit limits for each; and then calculated my debt-to-credit ratio. My Equifax report also tallied my monthly payment amounts in each category (mortgage, installment, and revolving debt) and informed me of how many accounts had a balance. So my point is simply this: Each credit report has something valuable to offer, but had I looked at only one report I wouldn't have learned as much.

To conclude, just because the TransUnion report didn't wow me visually doesn't mean that it wasn't valuable. Some people like to see information presented in a text-heavy manner with lots of explanations; others prefer charts and graphs; and still others like pictures or snapshot summaries. No matter what your preference, you'll be all the more educated about your credit if you take the time to look at the information contained in each of the three reports together. As proof of this, I should note that, despite my previous comments about the TransUnion report, I learned several valuable things from it. For instance, TransUnion was the only bureau to give me a summary of my credit history's length. At the top of my TransUnion report was the statement, "You have been on our files since 02/1987." This was good to know, especially since the length of credit history counts in computing one's score. The TransUnion report also explained a few mysterious codes that are sometimes contained in reports but not always explained.

4. More Comprehensive View of Your Overall Credit Standing

When you get all three of your credit reports at once, you're giving yourself the same comprehensive, birds-eye view of your credit profile that many lenders use. When banks are evaluating you for a major loan, such as a mortgage, many will pull a tri-merged report containing information from TransUnion, Equifax, and Experian. There's a reason why lenders want to look at all three of your reports—namely, to have the broadest possible look at your credit rating. If lenders and creditors take that full-scale approach to examining your credit, so should you. Some of you might ask, "But what if I'm not seeking a mortgage? Do I really need to know what's in all three reports?" The answer is a resounding yes. Even though you may not be in the market for a mortgage, is it possible that in the near future you will apply for any form of credit whatsoever—say a credit card, student loan, car loan, or line of credit? If so, you know that a bank is going to pull your credit. But the problem is that you don't know exactly which credit file they'll examine. That's why you should already know what's in all three of those reports. Don't take the risk of being ignorant about something missing or erroneous being in your credit file and having that information hurt your chances of getting the credit you want or need.

I hope that I've convinced you of the merits—indeed, the necessity—of getting all your credit reports at once. A simultaneous examination of all three files is a sure-fire way to get a true picture of your credit status. Given these facts, it's almost unthinkable that many people choose not to pull their credit files, even though they can get them quickly, free of charge, and conveniently online. Some statistics indicate, astonishingly, that one out of four adults has never seen a credit report.

The Law That Gives You a Free Credit Report—Again and Again and Again

Let's assume that you have taken advantage of your federal right to see your credit files via www.annualcreditreport.com. Did you know that in addition to that once-a-year deal you can get free credit reports again and again and again—multiple times in a year, if you like—online and directly from the credit bureaus? You can receive your reports at no cost and with zero obligation. It's true.

Here's a little-known piece of information you've probably never been told. Under a federal law called the Fair Credit Reporting Act, whenever you review your credit reports for inaccuracies in order to dispute any erroneous or outdated information in your files, each reporting agency—Equifax, Experian, and TransUnion—must allow you access to your current credit file at no charge whatsoever. I'm living proof of this fact.

In the summer of 2009 I retrieved all three of my credit reports via www.annualcreditreport.com. Then in October 2009 I went to the bureaus' websites and got free copies of my reports again simply by requesting them for the purpose of initiating a credit dispute with each bureau. The following month I disputed more information and got additional free reports. Mind you, these were legitimate disputes, but I point this fact out because the online dispute process is a loophole in the law to which most consumers seem to be completely oblivious. So if you've got faulty information on your credit report, don't pay for your files over and over again. Consider the response from TransUnion (they even used capital letters to highlight it) when I requested a report from that bureau to initiate an online credit dispute: "YOU ARE NOT REQUIRED TO PURCHASE ANY PRODUCT OR SERVICE, OR TO AGREE TO RECEIVE ANY INFORMATION OR MARKETING MATERIALS, TO USE THIS ONLINE DISPUTE SERVICE."

Here is something else to consider. I do not suggest abusing the system and randomly pulling credit reports every month just for the heck of it. Nevertheless, there is certainly nothing to prevent you from making legitimate requests for your credit reports in order to dispute false, inaccurate, or outdated data. If you dispute information online, you'll find that the credit bureaus require that you have already received a recent credit file, usually one less than 60 or 90 days old. After you acquire a free credit report to dispute erroneous data, if your review of your file turns up no mistakes, then you obviously do not need to dispute anything with the credit bureau. You still have the benefit of examining your file absolutely free. Moreover, you'll be provided with an up-to-date credit file any time you do this. If a credit bureau updates your file after you've successfully reconciled a dispute, by law it must give you a free report then too.

The Unemployed and Those Rejected for Credit Also Qualify for Free Reports

In addition to the online dispute process, certain consumers are entitled to a free credit report if they meet other criteria. By law you qualify for a free report any time a company takes "adverse" action against you based, at least in part, on information it got from your credit file. In layman's terms this means that any time you get turned down for employment, insurance, or credit, you are eligible for a free copy of your credit report, provided that you ask for it within 60 days of receiving that adverse notification. If you are denied something based on your credit standing, the company rejecting you will send a letter telling you which credit reporting agency (or agencies) they used to evaluate your credit history. You then can contact that bureau and ask for a credit report, even if you've already received a free report for the year. What's more, if you fit into any of these other categories, you can also get a free credit report:

⇨ You are receiving public assistance.
⇨ You have been a victim of identity theft.
⇨ You are unemployed and plan to seek a job within the next 60 days.
⇨ You reside in a state or territory (CA, CO, CT, GA, MA, MD, ME, MN, NJ, VT, USVI) that offers a free or reduced-priced credit report.

By my estimation more than 60 million Americans fit into the first three categories, making them eligible for free credit reports. After all, the number of Americans receiving food stamps (public assistance) recently hit a record 36 million; some 10 million people a year are victimized by identity theft; and there are approximately 15 million unemployed adults in the United States.

To get your free credit reports based on any of the circumstances mentioned above, or to initiate a credit dispute with the bureaus, use the following contact information for each credit-reporting agency. For fastest results, reach the bureaus online:

⇨ http://www.Equifax.com/fcra or http://www.investigate.equifax.com
By phone call 877-576-5766 for a free report or 888-800-8859 for a dispute.
By mail send your dispute to:
Equifax Information Services, LLC
Post Office Box 740256
Atlanta, GA 30374

⇨ http://www.Experian.com/reportaccess or http://www.Experian.com/disputes
By phone call 888-397-3742 for a free report or 866-200-6020 for a dispute.
By mail send your dispute to:
Experian
Post Office Box 9556
Allen, TX 75013

⇨ http://www.annualcreditreport.transunion.com/tu/disclosure/disclosure.jsp or
http://www.Transunion.com/investigate
By phone call 800-888-4213 for a free report or 800-916-8800 for a dispute.
By mail send your dispute to:
TransUnion Consumer Solutions
Post Office Box 2000
Chester, PA 19022-2000

Tip: Because Web links frequently change, if you go to any of the sites and can't find what you're searching for, type phrases such as "Free Credit Report," "Denied Credit," or "Credit Dispute" into their search boxes, and you should be able to track down what you need.

The point I'm trying to stress is that, even if you have already gotten your free annual reports via www.annualcreditreport.com but want to check your files again for any reason, you have a few options. Some of you may be thinking, "Why would I want or need to check my credit files more than once per year?" Here are some possible reasons:

⇨ You are applying for a loan and want to review your credit.

⇨ You are seeking a new job or promotion and know an employer will check your credit.

⇨ You want to monitor your credit for signs of identity theft.

⇨ You are trying to rent an apartment and need to know your credit standing.

⇨ You want to dispute an error in your credit file or have already done so and need to ensure that the mistake was fixed by the credit bureau(s).

How to Get Free Credit Reports from Other Companies in the Credit Industry

After you've exhausted your free credit-report options via www.annualcreditreport.com and have received any complimentary reports for which you may be eligible, you can still snag additional reports or summaries of your files without forking over any money. Simply use the no-cost offerings provided by companies such as FreeCreditReport.com, Quizzle.com, CreditKarma.com, Credit.com, or Zendough.com. Many more firms offer free credit reports too. I've received free credit reports and summaries from each of these organizations and can attest to their ease of use.

FreeCreditReport.com, for example, will provide a complimentary copy of your Experian credit report when you sign up for the company's monthly credit-monitoring service. Is this a good deal? Actually yes, mainly because everyone should have credit monitoring. If you don't want this service, however, simply call FreeCreditReport.com within a seven-day trial period to cancel, and you'll pay nothing. Either way, you still get the free Experian credit report.

Quizzle.com also offers consumers a free credit report from Experian. In fact, Quizzle provides you with a complimentary copy of your Experian credit file every six months, and no credit monitoring or trial subscription is required.

With CreditKarma.com and Credit.com you don't get an actual credit report. However, each company does give you a "Credit Report Card," which is a snapshot of your TransUnion file, in condensed format along with a letter grade of A, B, C, D or F to summarize your credit health in various areas.

Lastly, at Zendough.com, which promises to help you achieve financial peace of mind and mastery over your credit, you can get a free copy of your three-bureau credit report (showing your complete files from Equifax, Experian, and TransUnion) when you sign up for the company's monthly credit-monitoring service. Again, if you choose not to keep it, simply cancel during the seven-day trial period and pay nothing. You still get all three of your credit reports at no cost.

Each of these websites is highly secure, uses encryption to safeguard your data, and also offers credit tips and tools to help you improve your credit rating. In case you're wondering how Quizzle.com or CreditKarma.com can afford to provide you with free credit reports, they sell advertising for such financial products as credit-monitoring, identity-theft services, home loans, and credit-card deals.

Beware When Buying a Credit Report

You can also buy credit reports directly from the three leading bureaus and elsewhere. The current cost for a report is $11 from Equifax, $11 from TransUnion, and $10 from Experian. Refer to each bureau's website for the latest prices, as they can change at any time. Remember also my previous advice to those of you who want your credit report to dispute information contained therein: Seek a free report from the bureaus via the online process.

If you buy a credit report, or get one from any other source besides the credit bureaus, I caution you to look closely at the details of any offer that comes your way. In fact, the Federal Trade Commission warns people against falling for con artists posing as representatives of www.annualcreditreport.com. In one of its publications titled "Building a Better Credit Report," the FTC says:

Annualcreditreport.com is the only authorized online source for your free annual credit report from the three nationwide consumer reporting agencies. Neither the website nor the companies will call you first to ask for personal information or send you an email asking for personal information. If you get a phone call or an email— or see a pop-up ad—claiming it's from annualcreditreport.com (or any of the three nationwide consumer reporting agencies), it's probably a scam. Don't reply or click on any link in the message. Instead forward any email that claims to be from annualcreditreport.com (or from any of the three consumer reporting companies) to spam@uce.gov, the FTC's database of deceptive spam.

The Credit Report You've Probably Never Heard Of

A lot of discussion throughout this book has been focused on the "Big Three" credit-reporting agencies: Experian, Equifax, and TransUnion. But have you ever heard of the fourth-largest credit bureau in America? It's a company called Innovis, and it too wields considerable influence in the world of credit.

Unlike the other bureaus that let you get your credit reports online, you can only call or write Innovis to get your report. To contact Innovis by phone, call 800-540-2505. When you call, an automated system will guide you through a series of questions, and your Innovis credit report will be sent to you in three to five business days. To request your report by mail, write to Innovis, Attention: Consumer Assistance, Post Office Box 1358, Columbus, OH 43216-1358. Innovis credit reports cost from $1 to $11, depending on where you live.

Getting Credit Scores Must Be on Your Must-Do List

After getting your credit reports, your next duty is to get your credit scores, starting with FICO®. You can also go to Fair Isaac's consumer web site, www.myfico.com, to get your credit reports along with your FICO® scores. FICO® scores, though, are not free; they cost $15.95 each. As of this writing, however, you can only get two of your FICO® scores, the ones based on your Equifax and TransUnion credit files. In February 2009 FICO® stopped selling scores in the wake of an ongoing legal dispute between the two companies. Experian still allows Fair Isaac to sell Experian-based FICO® scores to lenders. However, Experian ended what had been a six-year agreement that previously allowed Fair Isaac to sell its linked FICO® scores to the public.

As mentioned, it costs $15.95 apiece to get your FICO® scores. Despite the cost I think that this is money well spent since Fair Isaac also gives you a range of credit-related tools and information to help you boost your credit score. To my mind it's always best to get information straight from the horse's mouth. And since the people at Fair Isaac are the dominant players in the credit-scoring world, it would be foolish to neglect an opportunity to get those scores. Some 98% of credit-card companies and 75% of mortgage lenders use FICO® scores as the basis for lending decisions. So get that credit report and those scores now.

Once you've gotten them, you should read the company's analysis of why your credit score is a certain number. Watch out for these types of negative statements:

⇨ Amounts owed on revolving accounts is too high
⇨ Amount past due on accounts
⇨ Serious delinquency, derogatory public record, or collection filed
⇨ Time since delinquency is too recent or unknown
⇨ Too many accounts with balances

Beyond late payments and other delinquencies, other reasons your FICO® score may take a hit are that you have too much debt outstanding, have too many recently opened accounts, or have a high number of credit inquiries. According to Fair Isaac, five criteria go into formulating your credit score: your payment history makes up 35% of your FICO® score; the amount of debt you owe comprises 30%; your length of credit history accounts for 15%; the existence of new credit makes up 10%; and the type of credit you're using constitutes the final 10%. Here is my own assessment of your credit based solely on your FICO® score as well as my personal and professional dealings with bankers and lenders of all kinds:

If your FICO® score is . . .	Then your credit is
760 - 850	Perfect
759 - 700	Good
699 - 650	Average
649 - 620	So-So
619 and below	Poor

I should note that before the credit crunch 620 was somewhat of a magic cutoff number. For example, many banks would require you to have a FICO® score of at least 620 in order to get a halfway decent mortgage rate. If your score was less than 620, could you still get the loan? Yes, in most cases, but depending on the severity of your credit problems, you had to pay a lot higher interest rate and more finance charges over the life of the loan. That's true at every level of the credit spectrum. Those in the "perfect" credit range will pay less than those with "good" credit; those with "good" credit will get better terms than people with "average" credit, and so on. In the current economic climate, having a FICO® score in the 600s, even the high 680s, could mean that your mortgage application gets denied.

Banks now want to see scores of 700 and higher, which is all the more reason to strive for perfect credit. I'm not saying that you won't get a loan if your scores fall below 700, but you should know that it's tougher, and you're likely to pay higher interest on any loans or credit you do receive if your credit rating isn't stellar.

Why You Need Your Experian PLUS Score Too

In addition to your FICO® scores, you should get your Experian PLUS score. In recent years consumers got all three FICO® scores based on their TransUnion, Equifax, and Experian reports, but as previously mentioned you now can get only two FICO® scores based on what's in your Equifax and TransUnion files. You no longer can get an Experian-based FICO® score. So what should you do to get a score based on all three credit files? My recommendation is to get your third credit score directly from Experian via its www.creditexpert.com consumer website. This score is known as your Experian PLUS Score. Some people suggest that buying any scores other than FICO® soley is not worth it. They contend that it's a waste of money to buy a score not used by lenders. However, I disagree. I think that it's ultimately far more valuable to have additional information, as opposed to less information, when it comes to your credit.

When you get your Experian PLUS score, you'll acquire keen insights into what is strengthening your credit profile and what is weakening it. Here's what Experian told me about my score, which was 780.

What Factors Raise Your PLUS Score?

⇨ You have paid your bills on time and currently do not have any overdue accounts or negative information such as a collection, charge-off, or bankruptcy on your report.

⇨ You have a good cushion of available credit between your current balance and your credit limits on all open trades. This has a positive effect on your credit score, showing lenders that you are unlikely to overextend yourself financially.

⇨ You have at least two active and major credit cards such as Discover, American Express, VISA, or MasterCard on your credit report. This tells lenders that you are a responsible borrower and good credit risk.

⇨ Your credit file shows no record of any current delinquencies on real-estate accounts such as a mortgage.

My Experian PLUS report also told me how my score stacked up against the rest of the U.S. population (I was in the 91st percentile), and it included a graph to illustrate how I would be viewed (High Risk, Medium-High Risk, Medium Risk, Medium-Low Risk, or Low Risk) if I were to change my payment patterns, credit usage, or other financial habits. I found all of these points relevant and useful.

Although the Experian PLUS score isn't the one pulled by lenders, it is nonetheless helpful. And for those who choose not to purchase their two FICO® scores, even though Experian uses a different scoring model than the one used to calculate your FICO® scores, knowing your Experian PLUS score gives you an approximation of how well you fare numerically based on information in your Experian file. For instance, the FICO® scoring model ranges from 300 to 850 points. By comparison, Experian's credit scores range from 330 to 830. When I purchased my Experian PLUS score, it was 780, roughly comparable to the level of my FICO® scores. So for the sake of having three scores, and getting deeper insights into your credit rating, I believe the Experian PLUS score is well worth its $14.50 price tag. Granted, it's not the score lenders use, but it's educational nonetheless.

The VantageScore Gains Modest Acceptance

There is a final credit score of which you should be aware. It's called the VantageScore, and it's a credit score jointly developed by the three credit bureaus. When I first wrote about VantageScores a few years ago, most experts suggested that consumers need not bother with these credit scores since lenders hadn't taken to using them. Amid the credit crunch, however, VantageScores have made headway in the financial world and now claim a 6% market share. That's small compared to the widespread use of FICO® scores, but it illustrates that increasingly banks are looking at alternative credit ratings—so perhaps you should too.

Upon launching VantageScores in March 2006, the "Big Three" credit-reporting companies promised that this new calibration would be more "accurate" than existing credit scores and would also ensure far less variance among the bureaus. For instance, one big complaint by consumers over the years is that they might get a credit score of 680 from Equifax, 710 from Experian, and 740 from TransUnion. With VantageScore consumers are supposed to benefit by getting scores that are more balanced because the three bureaus all use the same methodology and coding to calculate credit scores. In addition, the "Big Three" came up with a new numerical and grading system to classify a person's credit, with scores ranging from 501 to 990 points. The breakdown for VantageScores looks like this:

Vantage Score	Grade	Risk Category
901 to 990	A	Super Prime
801 to 900	B	Prime Plus
701 to 800	C	Prime
601 to 700	D	Non-Prime
501 to 600	F	High Risk

Collaborating in this fashion to come up with the VantageScore raised many eyebrows. Some critics and consumer groups questioned whether these credit agencies were guilty of anti-trust violations. Even though the credit bureaus sold and marketed VantageScores on their own, consumer advocates didn't like the fact that these business competitors had secretly teamed up to come up with a new product.

The U.S. Justice Department launched an informal inquiry into the matter. That inquiry was closed in February 2007, with no action being taken against the credit bureaus, but as of this writing the legal wrangling is ongoing. Fair Isaac, developer of the rival FICO® credit score, filed a federal anti-trust and trademark lawsuit against the three credit bureaus and VantageScore Solutions LLC in October 2006. (Equifax was later dropped from the lawsuit). In any event Fair Isaac lost that lawsuit in November 2009 when a federal jury ruled in favor of its competitors. Fair Isaac's lawsuit had alleged trademark infringement, as well as unfair and anti-competitive practices, but the jury didn't buy it, and neither did a U.S. District Judge who in July 2009 had dismissed Fair Isaac's anti-trust, breach of contract, and false advertising claims. Fair Isaac says that it will appeal both decisions.

Some experts think that Fair Isaac's losing its lawsuit may open the door for VantageScores to become even more popular with banks and consumers. In an interview in 2009, Barrett Burns, CEO of VantageScore Solutions LLC, told me, "We're still working hard on adoption," or getting banks to use the VantageScore model. Burns added that "the credit bureaus are responsible for all the sales activity" to the public. According to Burns, consumers can buy VantageScores from Experian and TransUnion but not from Equifax, due to Equifax's longstanding exclusive contract with Fair Isaac, creator of the FICO® score.

When asked what makes a VantageScore better or different from a FICO® score, Burns ticked off a host of reasons. He said that VantageScores are more predictive of risk because they emphasize recent consumer behavior and utilize insights gleaned during the credit crunch, as opposed to FICO®'s classic model based on older consumer data. Burns also asserted that VantageScores do a better job of scoring more people and capturing a broader array of payment information. For instance, if a consumer has utility-bill payments reported anywhere, that history is taken into account even though it's not a traditional form of credit. "Those data sources are extremely predictive. So we will score that if it's in a consumer file," Burns said. The VantageScore methodology, Burns added, helps "infrequent credit users, who tend to be the under-banked, the underserved, sub-prime, new credit users, and those with thin files." In addition, "FICO® doesn't score in the first six months of credit usage," Burns said. "We score as soon as a trade line comes into the credit bureau."

A trade line is simply an itemized listing or summary of a credit or financial account.

If you decide to get a VantageScore, the current cost for one is $7.95. To learn more about this credit score through each of the credit bureaus, go to:

http://www.Equifax.com/VantageScore/Consumers.html
http://www.VantageScore.Experian.com
http://www.TransUnion.com

Chapter 6:
Examine Your Files and
Enroll in Credit Monitoring

Once you get your credit report, it's up to you to interpret what's in there, which can sometimes be confusing. It may sound like a given, but you must actually *read* your reports because, believe it or not, many people who get their credit reports fail to go through them. Some may simply be checking a task off their list. Others may say, "Oh, I'll get to that later." Or perhaps some think, "This is going to take a while. Let me go through it when I have the time." Well, if you constantly put it off, you know what's going to wind up happening? You'll never get around to delving through those credit files, much like people who buy books and magazines and never read them. Don't let that happen with your credit reports.

The second step in achieving Perfect Credit is actually a two-part move. It's about examining your files and then examining them on a regular basis by enrolling in credit monitoring. In the first half of this chapter I will walk you through how best to analyze your reports. Then in the second half I will discuss everything you need to know about credit monitoring.

What to Expect in Your Credit Reports

When you take the time to examine your credit files, you will probably notice that there are differences among your three credit reports. Perhaps there's a charge account on one report that isn't showing up on the other two, or maybe the mortgage on your old house is showing a balance when it should have been reported as paid off. At this point you want to get a snapshot of how you are viewed by the rest of the lending and financial world. Are there any negative items such as late payments? What about liens or judgments against you? These are obviously red flags that hurt your credit reputation considerably. Or perhaps you have lots of accounts with small balances. For some lenders that may be a negative because having "too much" access to credit means you could go out and run up a boatload of bills.

Once you start scrutinizing your credit reports, you may feel as if you're trying to read tea leaves, but the process needn't be cryptic. For starters, let me tell you about the information you'll find in all credit files, regardless of whether they're from Equifax, Experian, or TransUnion. In addition, I will highlight some of the differences between each credit bureau's reports, pointing out where each one excels or offers unique insights into your credit profile.

All credit reports contain basic information that can be categorized into five groups: personal information, summary of accounts, public records, inquiries, and consumer statements. Let's consider what you may encounter in each area.

Personal Information: Make Sure It's Letter-Perfect

The top part of your credit report contains a condensed set of personal facts about you, the totality of which is extremely important in establishing your identity. The first, and most obvious, piece of information here will be your legal name. Make sure that it is spelled properly, and that goes for your first name, last name, and middle name if it's listed. If only your middle initial is listed, ensure that is correct too. You don't want to get your identity confused with someone else's, especially if you have a somewhat common name such as Mary Johnson. You also want to avoid being mistaken for another family member. An example of how this might occur is the case of a father and son who share the same name and live in the same city, perhaps even in the same home. One might have squeaky-clean credit, and the other might be a credit catastrophe. Needless to say, you don't want your credit reputation potentially tarred by someone else's bad credit.

Obviously, however, your full name alone isn't sufficient to verify your identity and distinguish you from someone else. That's why other bits of personal information are located in the first part of your credit report, including your date of birth, other names you have used (such as your maiden name), current address, previous addresses, home telephone number, and place of employment. Some reports will also include the last four digits of your Social Security number and the name of your spouse. Review the dates shown on your report that indicate how long you have lived at your current residence and how long you have worked at your present place of employment. While this information will not impact your credit score, it does send a message to potential creditors and others about how "stable" you've been. There's a reason banks, prospective employers, landlords, and others ask how long you've held a certain job or lived at your current residence. In general, showing continuity and stability in your work and home life is viewed more favorably than changing jobs and residences year after year. So you want the residency and employment dates on your credit report to be accurate.

If you have ever legally changed your name after marriage, divorce, or for any other reason, you are likely to see multiple names listed in your credit file. In addition, let me warn you that it is not uncommon to see a variety of spellings for your name. I'm always shocked when I see my updated credit files because there is invariably a ridiculous number of "aliases" contained in my report. (Believe it or not, in the past some credit reports actually used that sinister-sounding term.) Today, if multiple names are listed in your credit files, your reports will typically include phrases such as "Names," "Other Names," or "Also Known As." Then listed will be those other names.

To minimize potential misidentification, I've disputed wrong names, and so should you. I also request that credit bureaus delete name variations in my credit file when the spelling of my name gets especially ridiculous, such as the time I was identified in my TransUnion report as "Ynette Khalfani." Nevertheless, I've come to accept that, at least in my case, there will probably always be some spelling errors or multiple names listed, mainly because creditors are listing them incorrectly. This is unfortunate and shouldn't be the case, but it happens all too often.

The Type of Information That Is Not in Your Credit Reports

While you will find a host of personal information detailed in your credit files, certain types of information about you are not contained therein. None of the following data will be noted in any of your credit files:

⇨ Your checking, savings, or investment accounts
⇨ Your credit score (though companies can sell you this information separately)
⇨ Your divorce records
⇨ Your ethnic background or race
⇨ Your gender
⇨ Your income
⇨ Your medical history
⇨ Your political affiliation
⇨ Your religion

Some of this information is omitted because federal laws prohibit the data from being noted in your credit files. Other information is not contained because it has no bearing on your credit rating and is not predictive of your ability to handle debt. One final bit of personal information that may be included in your credit report is data about criminal records. Potential employers, creditors, and others who see your credit files can find out about any arrests or criminal convictions in your past. Under the Fair Credit Reporting Act, arrest records must be removed from your credit files after seven years. However, criminal convictions may be noted indefinitely in your credit reports.

Summary of Your Credit Accounts: The Good, the Bad, and the Ugly

The meat of your credit report will be a detailed listing of the open and closed accounts that creditors have reported about you. In this section you can find the following types of accounts (including current accounts or those you've had in the past):

⇨ mortgages
⇨ home-equity loans/lines of credit

⇨ credit cards
⇨ charge cards
⇨ department store or retail accounts
⇨ personal lines of credit
⇨ student loans
⇨ auto loans
⇨ medical-related debt
⇨ personal loans/notes
⇨ other accounts

Each account will be identified by an account name, meaning the creditor you owe, and an account number. The first few digits or the last few digits of your account numbers are frequently omitted to guard your privacy. (Some credit reports even scramble account numbers.) So don't worry about the account numbers too much at this phase, unless the account number, or the account itself, is totally unrecognizable to you.

What to Look for First in Your Summary of Accounts: Payment Status

For now the most important entries in this section of your credit reports are the "Status" references to whether you've paid your debts on time or been late and, if so, how late. This is where you should start as you delve into your account summaries.

Your payment history is shown as "Account Status," "Current Status," "Pay Status," or simply "Status." Open accounts with no delinquencies will have these types of "Status" comments: "Pays As Agreed," "Never Late," or "Current." Closed accounts with a positive credit history will be marked "Paid As Agreed" or "Pays As Agrees." Negative information will most commonly be indicated as 30-, 60-, 90-, or 120-day late payments. Other negative comments include "Collections," "Settled," or "Paid, Was 60 Days Late." If an account has been "charged off" or written off by a creditor as uncollectible, that fact will be noted too, typically along with the dollar amount charged off. In short, any notation in your credit file that you did not pay your debts exactly as originally agreed will be viewed negatively by credit-scoring firms and potential lenders.

The Dollar Balances Shown on Your Credit Reports

Other key data to examine pertains to the dollar amounts shown on each of your credit accounts. For each account you should see summaries of the following:

⇨ **Credit Limit/Original Amount**
This should reflect the amount of credit you were granted when the account was first opened.

⇨ **High Balance**
This figure should show the highest amount of credit you've ever used for each account.

⇨ **Balance or Recent Balance**
This dollar amount will indicate the last balance owed on this account as reported by your credit grantor. Frequently this information can be a month or so old. It depends on when you made your last payment, when your creditor reported an up-to-date balance to the credit bureaus, and when your credit report was actually pulled.

⇨ **Recent Payment**
This figure shows the most recent dollar amount that you paid on the account as reported by a creditor.

⇨ **Monthly Payment**
For mortgage debt or installment loans, this number should show your normally scheduled payment amount. For revolving debt (i.e., credit cards) it will indicate your minimum payment due.

Time-Related Information in Your Credit Files

In addition, your credit reports will contain time-related information about your accounts, specifically how long they've been open and when the most recent data about your payment history was collected. Expect to see the following:

⇨ **Date Opened**
This refers to the month and year in which you were approved for credit.

⇨ **Reported Since**
This date will be the first time the creditor began reporting an account to the credit bureaus. Sometimes this will match the "Date Opened," but in other instances it could be a month or a few months later.

⇨ **Date Reported, Date Updated, or Date of Status**
This refers to the most recent month and year that your creditor reported information about your account. For open accounts it may be the current month, or it could be a month or two old. For closed accounts it should be the date the account was paid off or closed.

⇨ **Date of Last Activity or Last Reported**
This date will correspond to the very last month that a creditor reported information about you or updated something in your credit file.

Creditor Descriptions of Joint and Individual Accounts

Lastly, in examining your credit files you will find descriptive information indicating the specific nature of your accounts, their repayment terms, and your level of ownership. This data will be reported under these headings:

⇨ **Type or Type of Account**
Home-related loans (including primary mortgages, home-equity loans, and any other loans based on real estate) will be described as "Mortgage." Credit cards and charge accounts will show up as "Revolving." Student loans and car loans should be referred to as "Installment." Certain retail charge accounts, for example at furniture stores, will be listed as "Open" accounts. Note also that sometimes mortgage-related accounts such as home-improvement loans will be listed as "Installment" debt. Home-improvement loans are sometimes categorized as "Installment" debt because you get a lump sum and

pay it down over time, just as with a car loan or student loan. Also, the balance on a home-improvement loan doesn't increase since you cannot tap it again and again.

⇨ **Terms or Term Duration**
This describes the repayment length, or payoff term, associated with each account. Most primary mortgages, for instance, will be noted as "30 Years." But if you had a shorter home loan, it could be shown as "15 Years." The "Terms" for credit cards may be noted as "Monthly" or "Due Every Month." In some cases credit-card and charge accounts will have an "NA" notation, or may simply be left blank, in the "Terms" section. Lenders and credit-scoring firms know that these are revolving accounts, and due every month, so having "NA" or a blank space in the "Terms" section will not harm you. Installment loans should state your scheduled repayment length. For example, a five-year car loan will have "60 Months" listed as its "Terms." A student loan with a 10-year payoff will have "120 Months" listed as its "Terms." Some credit reports also include the amount of your scheduled monthly payment. For instance, a mortgage may be listed as "$2,580 for 360 Months."

⇨ **Responsibility or Account Owner**
In this area your creditors will typically describe the account in question as one of the following: "Individual Account," "Joint Account," "Authorized User," "Participant on Account," "Shared," or "Shared, But Otherwise Undesignated."

Other Notations Contained in Your Account Summary Section

Comments in your credit file to look out for are:

⇨ **Dispute statements**
If you have disputed any information contained in your credit files, you will likely see a notation such as "Account information disputed by consumer."

⇨ **Account closure statements**
These are typically described as either "Account closed at consumer's request" or "Account closed by credit grantor." Be sure these statements are accurate.

⇨ **Status notations and statements**
These descriptions can be anything from "Open/Never Late" or "Open/30 Days Late" to "Closed/Paid As Agreed," "Closed/Charged Off," or "Collections."

When examining your credit history, don't be alarmed if you see very old information in your file, unless it's negative information that should have fallen off your credit report. For open accounts with positive payment histories, these listings will remain in your credit file for as long as they are open. Once you pay off an account, or once it is closed either by you or a creditor, that account will stay on your credit report for ten years. For instance, assume that you opened a credit-card account in 1999, then paid off the card and closed the account in 2005. That account will remain on your credit report until 2015. The presence of this account in your credit file actually helps you because, remember, part of your credit score is based on the length of your credit history. The further back your credit history goes, the better it is for your credit score.

Public Records in Your Credit Files

Although the Account Summary section of your credit reports will list negative information such as late payments or collections, more serious delinquencies will be contained in the "Public Records" area of your files. Here you will find:

⇨ **Judgments**
A judgment is a court verdict ordering you to pay an outstanding debt. If you get a judgment "Dismissed," you will almost certainly improve your credit rating because "Dismissed" court judgments are treated as if they never occurred. Wage attachments or garnishments may also appear as judgments. Unpaid child-support obligations that are seriously in arrears will often appear on a credit file. Usually these

are documented when a person was supposed to pay child support via a county or state agency but failed to do so for at least several months, sometimes for years, ultimately resulting in a court judgment against the individual. Judgments for delinquent child-support payments severely tarnish your credit rating and could result in wage garnishments and other actions being taken against you.

⇨ **Tax Liens**

Unpaid taxes owed to local, state, or federal authorities may show up on your credit file as tax liens. These typically stay on your Equifax and TransUnion files indefinitely until paid. Unpaid tax liens will remain on your Experian report for 15 years. (There is one exception. For residents of California, unpaid tax liens remain on their credit reports for only ten years).

You can expect a tax lien to cause a very large drop in your credit score, and it doesn't matter whether the amount owed was $150 or $150,000. A tax lien is a tax lien. Details such as where the court records are held, the case number, and the amount of taxes owed do not impact your credit score. Once paid off or satisfied, tax liens remain on your credit reports for seven years.

⇨ **Bankruptcies**

Although a bankruptcy is a way of legally discharging debts, it is also perhaps the most negative mark you can have on your credit. Bankruptcies generally remain on your credit report for ten years. After that time they should drop off your credit file and have no impact on your score. Note that, according to FICO®, a bankruptcy that is "Dismissed" does not lower your FICO®score. This is because a "Dismissed" bankruptcy basically wipes the slate clean and is regarded by credit-scoring firms as if the bankruptcy never happened. You will find your bankruptcy status under a reference to its "Disposition." Check that the "Date Filed" for any bankruptcy is accurate. This matters greatly for your credit rating because the more recent a bankruptcy the more it will negatively impact your credit rating. Lastly, while other details about a bankruptcy such as the court involved, the case number, or the type of bankruptcy filing (Chapter

7 or Chapter 13) do not impact your credit score, you should nevertheless try to ensure that this data is also reported correctly.

Credit Hunters: Watch Out for Excessive Inquiries in Your Credit Reports

An inquiry in your credit file is a record of any application for credit that you made. For example, if you seek a mortgage or car loan, or even if you apply for a credit card or perhaps request an increase in your current credit-card limit, any of these actions can result in an inquiry. Other business-related transactions can also produce inquiries, among them signing a cell-phone contract, launching new service with a utility provider, filling out an apartment rental application, and, as I described in a previous chapter, using a debit card to reserve or pay for a car rental. All of these activities generate inquiries that are known as "hard" pulls. By contrast, when you examine your own credit report, or when an existing creditor does a review of your credit files, those are called "soft" pulls, and they do not impact your credit score.

Credit-scoring firms typically describe inquiries as having a "modest" impact on your credit score. But what's so modest about a drop of up to 35 points in your FICO® score? That's what the American Bankers Association says a single inquiry can cost you. By Fair Isaac's own formula, inquiries account for 10% of your score. So think about it this way: If your FICO® score is 680 points, inquiries account for 68 of those points. Obviously it's not that simple because different elements of FICO's formula are weighted differently, and inquiries can have a greater or lesser impact on your score depending on the length of your credit history and other factors.

Nevertheless, to minimize the impact of inquiries on your credit rating, only apply for credit when you truly need it. And if you have to shop around for a mortgage or car loan, do so within a concentrated period of time. FICO® executives say that multiple inquiries for auto financing or home loans are treated as a single inquiry, so long as the inquiries all occur within a 14-day period. The idea, according to FICO®, is to avoid penalizing consumers for shopping around for the best rate. Inquiries generally stay on your credit report for two years, and they count against you in calculating your FICO® scores for one year.

Consumer Statements in Your Credit Files

Under the Fair Credit Reporting Act you are allowed to add a 100-word "Consumer Statement" to any of your credit reports if you have disputed an item in your credit files, but the item was not removed because it was verified by a creditor. Frequently consumers think that taking advantage of this "right" to add a consumer statement is a good opportunity. After all, you get a chance to divulge what happened, elaborate on the dispute, or perhaps explain why going through a divorce resulted in your not paying a bill. Perhaps you think that your explanation will prove that something wasn't your fault, or at the very least that a statement might show a lender that you had a "good" reason for failing to pay. Well, the truth of the matter is that from a lender's standpoint, especially in today's economic environment, there is not a single reason under the sun that can justify something negative in your credit report. Creditors want to know whether you paid your debts as agreed or not. Period. So don't fool yourself into thinking that your consumer statement will be "taken into account." It won't. In fact, your 100-word statement will most likely be viewed as confirmation that you were financially irresponsible, perhaps because you didn't manage your finances in such a way as to weather some unexpected event such as divorce or a layoff. A consumer statement, in short, lumps you in the same category with all the other credit-damaged individuals who are using such statements to plead their case.

So my advice is simple: Refrain from putting any statement at all on your credit file. For those of you fretting over something in your credit file, and worried that it may damage your chances of getting a needed loan, fear not. When you apply for a loan of any kind, chances are that it will be approved or denied solely based on numbers—not words. The numbers will be things like the following: What is your FICO® score? How much debt are you carrying? What is your income? If your application is truly in a gray area, and potential lenders have questions about your credit history, rest assured that they'll ask if they need more information from you in order to approve your loan. And at that point you can write a letter directly to that lender succinctly explaining anything you feel is necessary. You don't need to put explanations in a credit report where scores of businesses will see it and may even view the consumer statement as proof that you aren't a good credit risk because you couldn't pay your bills on time.

There is another practical reason why you should avoid consumer statements: They remain on your credit reports for ten long years. Assume that you had a dispute with a creditor and, through your perseverance or some settlement, you resolved the matter. The dispute is over. The creditor may even agree to delete negative information, change your payment status, or update your credit history, all of which could wipe away any reference to the matter. But if you have that consumer statement still lingering in your credit file, it will be a "heads up" to potential lenders that at one point you were late with a bill or had some dispute with a creditor. It's worse if you have a late payment or a negative account several years old. If the blemish on your record occurred, say, four years ago, it will come off your credit file in another three years. However, if you added a consumer statement perhaps just a year ago, then the statement referencing the black mark on your credit will remain another nine years—six years longer than the late payment itself was shown!

Hopefully your credit reports currently indicate: "There is no consumer statement associated with this file," or something to that effect. If not, you can dispute an existing consumer statement, or simply write a letter to the credit bureaus, and try to get it deleted. For example, TransUnion allows individuals to write a letter to add or remove a consumer statement from its credit reports. To get a consumer statement removed, send a consumer-statement removal request, along with your name, address, and File Identification Number, to TransUnion Consumer Relations, Post Office Box 2000, Chester, PA 19022. If you write the credit agencies to delete a consumer statement and the request is denied, be prepared to wait it out until any statement you supplied to the bureaus eventually expires.

Key Differences among Equifax, Experian, and TransUnion Credit Reports

I have explained the common type of information you can expect to find in all your credit reports, regardless of whether you pull an Equifax, Experian, or TransUnion credit file. To recap, that data includes five areas: personal information, summary of accounts, public records, inquiries, and consumer statements. At this point let me describe some of the key differences you will encounter as you examine your three credit reports.

⇨ **Equifax Highlights**

As of this writing, Equifax reports are the only ones that summarize "Open Accounts" and "Closed Accounts," making it far easier to distinguish this information and choose which accounts you want to address first. (With Experian and TransUnion, all accounts are grouped together and listed alphabetically). Equifax files also often show an 81-month credit history for your accounts. In some cases, however, particularly for closed or paid accounts, you will see a statement saying: "No 81-Month Payment Data Available for Display."

⇨ **Experian Highlights**

Experian credit reports contain a unique feature that many users find extremely enlightening. For all of the accounts listed in your credit file, Experian shows you "Status Details" indicating when an account is scheduled to fall off your credit report. For example, an auto loan that you paid off and closed in July 2008 will show the following information: "This account is scheduled to continue on record until July 2018." Or let's say you had an account go to collections and ultimate get written off by a creditor. For those of you who with these and other negative marks in your credit file, you won't have to wonder how long a certain blemish will haunt you. That critical "Status Details" section of your Experian report will give you the precise information.

With Experian credit files you will also see a "Balance History" for any accounts that are still open or for those closed accounts with an outstanding balance. The "Balance History" information in Experian reports currently dates back to November 2007. Also included in the "Balance History" section will be a statement indicating what your high credit/high balance has been, over different time frames, since November 2007. If you have accounts opened after November 2007, the "Balance History" data will reflect whatever time period you opened the account. For instance, it could say: "Between September 2008 and March 2010 your credit limit/high balance was $5,000."

⇨ **TransUnion Highlights**

TransUnion has the most thorough employment data section in your personal summary. You can update or correct several fields, including your current or previous employer's name as well as the position you held and the date of your being hired. Again, this information will not improve your credit score. However, if you ever seek a loan in the future, it will be helpful to have your information reflected accurately in your credit report to show a lender your hire date for a job or the length of time you spent at a specific employer.

TransUnion reports list "Satisfactory" and "Unsatisfactory" accounts. They also include color-coded boxes (white, green, yellow, orange, and red) with words or numbers inside them to indicate your payment history:

* A white box with an "X" indicates unknown information.
* A green box with "OK" signals that your payment is current.
* A yellow box with "30" means that you were 30 days late on a payment.
* An orange box with "60" means that you were 60 days late.
* A red box with "90" means that you were 90 days late.
* A red box with "120" means that you were 120 days late.

Lastly, TransUnion also uses the notation "N/A" or "Not Applicable" to describe various accounts.

What Do All Those Strange Codes in My Credit Report Mean?

While examining your credit reports, you may also see a hodgepodge of codes or letters, especially in the inquiries section, indicating who has seen your credit files. These are abbreviations that reference some factoid in your credit file. Among the most common codes pertaining to inquiries are the following:

Code/Abbreviation: Meaning of Code

PRM: Inquiries with this prefix indicate that only your name and address were given to prospective credit grantors so that they can provide you with a firm offer of credit or insurance (PRM inquiries remain active for twelve months).

AM or AR: These inquiries are initiated by one of your creditors as a routine review of your credit file. Any AM and AR inquiries will be reported on your credit file for 12 months.

EMPL: Inquiries with this prefix indicate an employment inquiry (EMPL inquiries remain active for 24 months).

PR: Inquiries with this prefix indicate that a creditor reviewed your account as part of a portfolio it was purchasing (PR inquiries remain active for 12 months).

Equifax or EFX: Inquiries with these prefixes indicate Equifax's activity in response to your contact for a copy of your credit file or a research request.

ND: Inquiries with this prefix are general inquiries that do not display to credit grantors (ND inquiries remain active for 24 months).

ND MR: Inquiries with this prefix indicate the reissue of a mortgage credit file containing information from your Equifax file transmitted to another company in connection with a mortgage loan (ND inquiries remain active for 24 months).

Your Credit Report: A Holiday Credit Quiz

Now that you've had a chance to scour your credit information, I'd like you to answer this question: If you had to classify your credit report as a holiday, what would it be? Something frightful like Halloween or maybe something more like Thanksgiving?

It's hard to know how you might react to seeing your credit report, especially if you're examining it for the first time. Some of us are shocked at the damage we've done with past financial mistakes. Others are elated to see a top-notch credit rating. In the interest of getting you to think about your credit all year long, think of the holidays that occur during various months of the year and then answer this question.

If you had to classify your credit report as a holiday, which one would it be?

Be sure to take the full Holiday Credit Quiz in Appendix C at the end of this book. Once you answer the question, write me at info@themoneycoach.net and let me know your response.

How Credit Monitoring Can Help You to Achieve Perfect Credit

For most of this chapter I have provided an overview of what to expect when initially examining your credit files. For the remainder I will explain why examining your credit reports continuously is necessary to achieve Perfect Credit. The best way you can examine your files on a regular and ongoing basis is to enroll in credit monitoring.

The Basics of a Credit-Monitoring Service

Credit monitoring is a fee-based service offered to consumers by credit-reporting agencies, credit-scoring firms, and other companies. While credit-monitoring firms offer an array of options, from updated credit reports and scores to legal protection against identity theft, their basic purpose is to act as a watchdog over your credit information. When you sign up for a credit-monitoring service, one or all of your credit reports are constantly tracked, and you are alerted to changes in your files. For example, if a balance on one of your credit cards suddenly surges by $1,000, a credit-monitoring service will so inform you. Or, if a creditor does a "hard" pull of your file, indicating that you are seeking credit or a loan, the service would notify you of that inquiry. If any negative information is reported about you by the bureaus, credit-monitoring immediately conveys that information as well.

Why the Critics Are Wrong about Credit Monitoring

Before I elaborate on how credit monitoring can help in your quest for top-notch credit, let me first address an opposing point of view. Specifically I want to offer my thoughts about advice you may have heard that you shouldn't bother with credit-monitoring services. In a nutshell the knock against credit monitoring has been threefold. Critics say it's costly, unnecessary, and ineffective in preventing identity theft. Let's evaluate each of these claims to see if they really hold water.

In terms of cost, the average credit-monitoring service runs about $14.95 per month or roughly $180 a year. That's not cheap, especially in an era when we're all watching our budgets, but I would argue that $180 a year isn't expensive either for something that can help you save thousands of dollars annually, and likely many tens of thousands or even hundreds of thousands of dollars over your lifetime. Consider just a single loan such as a mortgage. Improving your credit score by 80 points, advancing from 680 to 760, will save you a $60 a month on a $250,000 mortgage, according to Fair Isaac. Based on prevailing interest rates in November 2009, a person with a 680 FICO® score would pay $1,338 a month (using a 4.974% interest rate), whereas a person with a 760 FICO® score would pay just $1,278 per month (assuming a 4.575% interest rate). Saving $720 a year on your housing cost is pretty impressive and definitely worth investing $180 annually in credit monitoring to help boost your credit scores.

Credit Monitoring Helps You Save Lots of Money

But the real payoff comes over time. Over the 30-year life of a mortgage, the person with a 760 FICO® score will save more than $21,000 in interest payments as compared with the individual with a 680 FICO® score. To be exact, $231,710 in interest payments would be made by the lower-score homeowner, while $210,036 in interest payments would be paid by the homeowner with the better score. Now think about all the loans you're likely to apply for in your life—credit cards, business loans, auto loans, mortgages, perhaps student loans, and so on. Toss in also all the car insurance and life insurance you'll buy throughout your life. Recall too my earlier story about Bill and Skip regarding how the person with Perfect Credit will save more than $1 million in a lifetime over the person with bad credit. Tally it all up, and it's clear that having the highest possible credit rating will save you a bundle. In this context credit monitoring is an investment. It's the price you pay to help you achieve Perfect Credit. And when you think about the potential cash you could squander by paying higher interest rates for having a less than stellar credit rating, credit monitoring is far from a waste of money. On the contrary, it's a bargain.

Credit Monitoring Is an Essential Credit-Management Tool in the New Economy

But what about those who contend that credit monitoring is "unnecessary" because you can get three reports via www.annualcreditreport.com and stagger those reports over time throughout the course of a year? Well, as explained earlier, you are at a serious disadvantage if you check only one credit report at a time, because you will invariably go for months before you discover what is contained in your other credit files. During that time lapse there could be errors in your reports that harm you financially or damage your reputation. Someone could have opened accounts in your name without your realizing it, or you may simply want regular and unfettered access to your reports without a lot of hassles. Credit monitoring will aid you in each of these instances. So the idea that credit monitoring is unnecessary is simply wrong-headed thinking, especially in an economic environment where your credit rating determines so many aspects of your life.

Credit Monitoring Helps to Detect and Minimize the Damage of Identity Theft

Let's look at the final reason that some experts don't like credit monitoring. They say it doesn't prevent identity theft. On this count I agree wholeheartedly. Credit monitoring doesn't prevent identity theft because nothing does! The fact is that if a con man is intent on stealing someone's private information, and misusing it in any way, no safeguards can stop such a thief. But even if credit monitoring doesn't *prevent* identity theft outright, that doesn't mean it can't help *detect* or *deter* it. So don't be swayed by the fallacious argument that credit monitoring is "useless" because it won't stop an identity thief. If we all followed that faulty logic, none of us would have alarms in our homes simply because an alarm doesn't *prevent* a thief from breaking into a residence. Alarm companies don't sell their wares by telling homeowners that alarms will keep a burglar from breaking a window, picking a lock, or gaining entrance via back doors. What they do tell homeowners, though, is that having an alarm service is a great defensive tool. Once that home alarm starts ringing, it will likely scare the thief off, hopefully leaving him little or no time to clean out your belongings. And even if a silent alarm is triggered, and the police are notified without the burglar's knowing it, the thief risks being caught because he doesn't realize that the authorities have been alerted.

Think about credit monitoring the same way. It won't stop the crooks, but it can give you an early warning of their activities, such as when an inquiry or new account mysteriously appears on your credit report or when an alert indicates your home address has been suspiciously changed. (Identity thieves often re-route mail in order to have your private information sent to them or to receive new credit cards they've applied for in your name.) If you receive a credit-monitoring alert warning you of any of these scenarios, you can act immediately to put a fraud alert or credit freeze on your files. Either of these measures will prevent additional credit's being extended to the identity thief, thus preventing further damage to your credit rating. So it's misleading to talk about credit monitoring as being a weak or ineffective method of *stopping* identity thieves altogether. Absolutely nothing does that.

Additional Benefits of Credit Monitoring

In addition to the three points outlined above, let me highlight eight other benefits of credit monitoring.

Updated Credit Reports and Scores
One of the benefits of credit monitoring is that you often receive additional credit reports and scores during the term of your monitoring plan. For example, FreeCreditReport.com offers its subscribers fresh credit scores twice a month, as well as unlimited access to their updated Experian reports any time consumers want them (even daily).

Improved Credit Education
Constantly reviewing your credit files and being aware of changes to

your credit profile promote enhanced financial literacy and better credit awareness. In addition, many credit-monitoring companies offer online resources including credit tips, articles, tools, and calculators to boost their subscribers' credit knowledge.

Legal Services and Insurance Protection

Most credit-monitoring services provide you with legal services and/or insurance, often to the tune of $50,000 or more, to help you clean up the mess that an identity thief might cause. LifeLock offers a $1 million service guarantee designed exclusively to cover the cost of lawyers, investigators, and case managers called upon to aid you. Equifax offers up to $1 million in identity-theft insurance.

Financial Reimbursements

If you are victimized by identity theft while you have credit monitoring in force, many firms will reimburse you for a variety of losses. For instance, a credit-monitoring company might pay you for lost wages, allow you to hire a private investigator at their expense, or provide you with reimbursements to cover out-of-pocket expenses, as well as any funds stolen from you or charges for which you might be held responsible.

Speedy Resolution of Errors

Credit monitoring offers you one of the fastest ways available to spot mistakes in your credit files as soon as errors occur. If you get a monitoring alert or simply catch an error as a result of constantly reviewing your credit reports, you'll be well positioned to dispute those errors promptly.

Early Notification of Adverse Creditor Actions

A common occurrence during the credit crunch has been the tendency of banks and other lenders to slash people's credit lines or close their accounts, often without informing the account holders. This trend has been especially vexing for infrequent credit-card users or those with "dormant" accounts. Unfortunately, the revelation about a reduced credit line or an inaccessible/closed account often comes when a person is trying to use the credit. Consumers with credit monitoring quickly learn of these account changes, even if their creditors don't immediately let them know. Since creditors typically report closed accounts to credit bureaus within a month of taking such action, an account closure would trigger a credit-monitoring alert to the consumer ("Account closed by credit grantor"), prompting that customer to contact the creditor for more information.

Automation of a Key Area of Personal Finances

For very busy individuals (and who isn't busy with an array of family, work, and other obligations?), credit monitoring takes a key area of your personal finances—the routine examination of your credit files—and puts it on autopilot for you. Just as online bill-payment services help people pay recurring debts automatically, so too does credit monitoring automate certain aspects of managing your credit. Instead of worrying about sending yourself emails, text messages, or other reminders, you are automatically provided with electronic credit updates to make the monitoring of your credit information a hassle-free process.

Peace of Mind is Priceless

One last benefit of credit monitoring deserves mention. For people who like the comfort of knowing that their credit files are being protected daily, credit monitoring is an indispensable way to ease worry about the unexpected. And for many individuals that peace of mind is priceless.

I have been using credit monitoring for more than five years. During that time staying on top of my credit has helped me to boost my scores; secure better rates on home loans, credit cards, and insurance; detect unauthorized inquiries into my credit files; and spot potentially damaging mistakes in my reports. Therefore, I can say without hesitation that all the credit-monitoring services I have paid for have been exceedingly worthwhile. They've also helped me to achieve and maintain Perfect Credit. I thus have no doubt that credit monitoring can do the same for you.

Chapter 7:
Reduce Debt and Manage Bills Wisely

As I previously indicated, there is a very strong link between your debt and your credit standing. Because your payment history—how good you are at paying bills on time—is the number-one factor in determining your FICO® scores, it's imperative that you take managing your debt very, very seriously. Start by doing whatever it takes never to miss a payment for any reason whatsoever. If you do that single thing, you'll start to increase your FICO® scores. If you've skipped or been late with payments in the past because money was tight, adjust your budget to ensure that you can faithfully pay every bill on time. And when I say "every bill," I mean exactly that. Don't neglect your light bill in the mistaken belief that a local energy service won't report your delinquent account to the credit bureaus. They can, and they will. The same is true for cell-phone providers, water companies, and public utilities. Don't believe for one minute that the only bills you have to keep up to date in order to protect your credit are your mortgage, car loan, and revolving accounts. These obligations should certainly take precedence over less urgent bills. Nevertheless, a 30-day late payment, even if it is just for a telephone bill, still looks bad on your credit report and will lower your credit score. Would you believe that in some parts of the country even parking tickets and overdue library fines are being reported to credit bureaus? It's true. Can you imagine being denied a bank loan, or having to get one at a higher rate, just because of a fine for failing to return a library book on time? As I said in the beginning, Perfect Credit is something you should constantly strive for, and being diligent in managing your bills is the chief way to do that.

With Americans owing more than $16 trillion in consumer debt, there's more opportunity than ever for people to mismanage their finances in ways that have a long-term impact on their credit health. Throw in the fact that financial literacy is not taught in this country, and you have a recipe for financial disaster. It's no wonder then that seven out of ten Americans, according to an Associated Press poll, feel as though their finances are out of control. All these factors demonstrate the need for solid credit and debt management.

Dealing with Debt Disease

In addition to being judicious about paying your current bills, you need to get serious about knocking out long-standing debt in order to boost your financial reputation and enhance your credit standing. Many of you have read one of my previous books titled *Zero Debt: The Ultimate Guide to Financial Freedom*. If so, you know that I consider excessive debt to be financial cancer. The focus of this chapter, therefore, is to give you strategies for eliminating debt, which in turn will boost your credit score.

I want you to recall, however, a critical point I made earlier in this book: All debt is not created equally, especially when it comes to credit scoring. Excessive credit-card debt is the worst of form of debt, and for good reason too. So to enhance your credit rating, use these three methods when tackling your debt:

⇨ Focus first and foremost on reducing credit-card debt.
⇨ Get strategic about lowering your credit-card utilization.
⇨ Fix other debt problems (e.g., student loans, car notes, mortgages, medical debt).

How to Eliminate Excessive Credit-Card Debt

I know from firsthand experience how stressful it can be to have a mountain of credit-card debt. Just thinking about the prospect of chipping away at that heap of debt can be exhausting. Perhaps you're frustrated that due to recent economic or personal circumstances you now suddenly find yourself in debt, even if previously you handled your financial affairs well. Or maybe you've been immersed in debt for so long that living on credit has become a way of life for you. No matter what your situation, take heart. You can slay the debt monster in your life just by applying some tried and true techniques used by people like myself who have successfully dug themselves out of credit-card debt. To get started, try these ten strategies:

⇨ Create a realistic budget.
⇨ Banish emotional spending.
⇨ Use financial windfalls properly.
⇨ Leverage the Internet to spend less.
⇨ Sell stuff you don't want, need, or use.
⇨ Turn a hobby into cash.
⇨ Adjust your withholdings at work.
⇨ Get a second job.
⇨ Squeeze money from your residence.
⇨ Start using cash more frequently.

Budget Is Not a Four-Letter Word

Despite what you've been told (or may feel), budget is not a four-letter word. When it comes to finances, I can think of no other word in the English language that evokes such disdain or opposition than the word "budget". Okay, maybe the word "taxes," but "budget" still ranks right up there.

Seven out of ten adults in America don't use a monthly budget. Little wonder, then, that so many people overspend and live beyond their means. To master your finances, including your credit, it's imperative that you get a handle on your expenses and compare that total to the net income you have coming in each month.

Until now it may be the case that no one ever explained to you how to create a budget. After all, budgeting isn't a skill taught in most homes or even in school. Or perhaps you've tried but just haven't been able to stick to a budget. Whatever the case may be, it's high time you learned six secrets to establishing a fool-proof budget, one that you can live with over time without feeling deprived and without worrying that unforeseen circumstances will wreck your finances. These six secrets, revealed below in a series of do's and don'ts, can help anyone become a whiz at budgeting.

Secret #1: Don't Let Misconceptions Hinder You

To master budgeting, you first have to change your mindset about what it means to live on a budget. Be honest: When you think about being "on a budget," do you inwardly loathe the idea, wishing instead you had so much money that you could spend on anything you want? Or do you automatically assume that having a budget means drastically changing your lifestyle because there will be a lot of things you can't buy, do, or have? If so, you must banish those negative thoughts and misconceptions. First of all, even millionaires have budgets. Realize also that creating a budget, and living within it, doesn't have to be unduly restrictive. Nor does it mean a complete end to all spending or having fun. In fact, a well prepared budget will have certain "treats" built into it. And it's precisely those "treats" that will help you stick to your budget. More on that later, but for now it helps to think about a budget as your personal "Spending Plan." With such a plan you establish priorities about what to do with your money—and what *not* to do with it. In other words, with a Spending Plan you'll no longer be making an endless series of impulse purchases. Instead, you'll finally control your money instead of letting your money control you.

Besides giving you power and control over your finances, a skillfully crafted budget:

⇨ Keeps you from living paycheck to paycheck.
⇨ Allows you to save for future goals and dreams.
⇨ Helps you avoid going into debt.
⇨ Reduces stress and worry about paying bills.

When you look at these benefits of having a budget or Spending Plan, it's clear that you should embrace the concept, not fret over it.

Secret #2: Do Make A List of *All* Expenses

An essential part of creating a budget is to list your bills, but many people unwittingly go astray during this step. Some individuals omit certain expenses, dismissing them as "one-time" expenditures, or maybe you forget about certain bills because they're paid semi-annually and not monthly.

To get a clear handle on your finances, you must include *all* expenses incurred during the year. Begin by itemizing all areas in which you regularly spend money. Some common categories include the following:

⇨ Food
⇨ Housing
⇨ Entertainment
⇨ Transportation
⇨ Debts
⇨ Utilities
⇨ Education
⇨ Insurance

Also add to your list any categories based on your personal lifestyle and circumstances. For instance, if you have children, you might include childcare or a category for gifts to celebrate birthdays, holidays, graduations, and other special occasions. Or maybe you're an avid reader. If so, include a category for magazine subscriptions or books. Your list of expenses can be written down or entered on a computer spreadsheet. The key is to capture accurately all your spending and calculate a monthly amount for each category. If you pay for something once a year, or even several times a year, simply add up the annual cost and divide it by 12 for a monthly sum. For example, assume that you pay $800 a year for auto insurance and that you typically pay the entire annual premium in December. Divide that $800 by 12, and you get an average monthly cost of about $67. That's the amount you should put aside in your budget each month for 12 months instead of trying to come up with $800 at year's end. A great way to keep tabs on everything, and learn to become a better saver and budgeter, is to use online tools. Several excellent resources include www.mint.com, www.budgettracker.com, and www.budgetpulse.com.

Secret #3: Don't Break the #1 Rule of Budgeting

The #1 rule of budgeting is this: *You cannot spend more than you earn.* Sounds simple enough, right? Well, unfortunately, most people don't follow this simple rule. Spending more than you earn violates a cardinal principle of good financial management because it means you're deficit-spending. Anyone who spends more than he or she earns each year, whether it's $20,000 or $20 million, will always be broke and in debt. So after you tally up all your expenses, you need to compare them against your net income or actual take-home pay. If your bills exceed your earnings, you must revamp your Spending Plan, giving priority to necessities. Start by cutting out luxuries first and then non-essential purchases to bring your spending in line with your income. No excuses. No exceptions.

Secret #4: Do Reward Yourself

Here's a little-known secret that successful budgeters use, especially those who have to revamp tight budgets because there are lots of bills to be paid. In order to stick to a budget over the long haul, successful budgeters give themselves "treats" along the way. These treats are financially planned, accounted for, and built into their budgets. Think of them as rewards for good financial behavior. Only you can decide what reward will make you happy and motivate you to stick to your budget. My recommendation is that you pick something of enduring value, not something frivolous. Let's say you enjoy a hobby such as photography. Build into your budget a monthly allotment for film, camera equipment, or maybe a photography class. By rewarding yourself with modest but meaningful treats, you won't feel as though you're being deprived while on a budget.

Secret# 5: Do Include a Savings Category in Your Budget

When you created your original list of expenses, did you include a savings category? Probably not. Most people omit savings from their budget, erroneously assuming that they can't "afford" to save or that there's simply not any money in the budget to save. This is a big financial mistake. Without regularly setting aside some savings, you're setting yourself up for budgeting failure. Any time something pops up (say you get a flat tire), you'll blow your budget or be forced to use a credit card. Do yourself a favor: Add a savings category to your budget, no matter how much or little you may have to save.

Secret# 6: Don't Forget to Plan for Some Budget-Busters

Savvy budgeters also know that unexpected events and emergencies will always occur, so they plan accordingly for contingencies to minimize their impact. If you own a home or car, calamities like a burst boiler unit or faulty engine can ruin a budget. Try to preempt such events by taking preventative measures, such as regularly servicing your boiler or having routine maintenance done on your car to avoid breakdowns and malfunctions.

If you follow these tips, you can easily create a livable budget, one that will help you to eliminate many worries about debt and get you on track to achieving Perfect Credit.

Are You Guilty of Emotional Spending?

If we're honest with ourselves, many of us will admit that so much of what we spend money on—and why we spend money—is tied to our emotional state. Sometimes we spend money completely on a whim because something struck us a being a "must have" item. At other times our purchasing decisions are wrapped up in the way we feel overall, and it may be a mood we've been in for weeks. We thus spend money for a host of reasons: boredom, depression, elation, or angst, just to name a few emotions. We also shop because we may want to reinforce our egos or simply because we feel as though we deserve something. The important point is to recognize when such emotional spending puts you in the red. What good is it to "feel like a million bucks," simply because you have the external trappings of success, when you're really a wreck about your finances? This is what emotional spending does. It makes you feel guilty about your purchases, and it sets you back financially.

Women are especially susceptible to shopping as a way to feel better. It's easy to engage in "retail therapy" if you're angry, depressed, or frustrated about something. Going on an emotional spending binge, however, is just as dangerous as going on a drinking binge: You may get a short-term sense of euphoria, but any emotional boost you experience will quickly give way to renewed feelings of guilt and despair. Moreover, you'll face the ultimate shopper's hangover—credit-card bills that take months to pay off. Read on to discover eight ways to stop engaging in "retail therapy."

Eight Ways to Stop Emotional Spending

Leave the credit cards at home

As a matter of practice, leave your credit cards at home more often than not. Having credit cards, charge cards, and department-store cards in your wallet or purse makes it easy to make spur-of-the-moment shopping trips. You'll think more about your spending practices if you have to part with your hard-earned dollars versus whipping out a credit card. Moreover, people tend to spend more when they use plastic instead of cash.

Use the "24-hour rule"

When you see something expensive that you think you "must" have, be willing to wait on that purchase for 24 hours and tell yourself that, if you still really want the item, you can always go back and get it the next day. In many cases that 24-hour period will be just the break you need not to indulge yourself.

Set a budget

For most shopaholics it's pointless to say, "Just don't shop!" If it were that easy, no one would have a shopping problem. The real issue isn't shopping in and of itself. The real issue is *excessive* shopping or compulsive, habitual, out-of-control shopping. Sometimes it happens at certain times of the year such as holidays. To combat the problem and keep your finances intact, give yourself permission to do some shopping—within reason. Set a realistic amount of money that you can spend each month without racking up debt. Once you hit your limit, do everything in your power to stop shopping for the rest of the month.

Enlist the help of friends and family

When you go on a shopping excursion, take a buddy with you who will not let you go overboard. That friend should know your budget or spending limit for that particular outing. Then it's the friend's job to get you out of the mall or away from the stores once you reach your limit. Also, tell any supportive family members that you're working on curbing your spending, and ask for their encouragement in helping you meet your goal.

Limit shopping trips to "emotion-neutral" times

Be aware of your emotional state at all times and pledge that you will not shop when your emotions are off kilter. This means foregoing shopping trips when you feel any kind of emotional extreme such as elation, sadness, or depression. If you must shop, do so during "emotion-neutral" times— i.e., when you're on a relatively even emotional keel.

Channel your energy

Find alternative things to do. Instead of hitting your favorite stores, channel your energy into more positive activities such as exercising, reading, or pursuing a hobby. If you're busy, especially if you're doing something fun and physical, you'll not only be too occupied to do mindless shopping but you'll also be engaged in a healthy, stress-busting activity.

Get to the root of the problem and recognize your emotional-spending "triggers"

You can also get a handle on impulse shopping binges by preventing them in the first place and learning why your spending is out of control. Start a journal. Write down what happens in your life and look for patterns to see whether something serves as a "trigger" event that makes you want to shop. Also, reflect about your past. Write down notes about when you first became a shopaholic, how shopping makes you feel, and what emotions you experience before and after you shop.

Join a support group for shopaholics

Lastly, for serious shopaholics, try joining a support group such as the Stopping Overshopping Program (www.StoppingOvershopping.com) created by April Lane Benson, Ph.D., the author of *I Shop, Therefore I Am: Compulsive Buying and the Search for Self.* Dr. Benson has been in private practice in New York City for nearly 30 years and has treated many women who are excessive shoppers. A similar program, is offered by psychotherapist Olivia Mellan, the author of *Overcoming Overspending.* She has teleclasses, CDs, books, and resources on her website (www.MoneyHarmony.com) to help shopaholics.

By getting to the root of why you consistently splurge, you'll understand how your habits first began and how to combat the cultural and media influences that make you want to hit the mall and shop unnecessarily or excessively.

Use Financial Windfalls Properly

Maybe it's not in the cards for you to become a multi-million dollar lottery winner, but that doesn't mean you won't come into a financial windfall. Such an unforeseen boon can help you to reduce credit-card debt and boost your credit rating as well. What qualifies as a windfall? It's any lump sum of money, expected or unexpected, beyond your normal paycheck. Examples of windfalls are life-insurance proceeds (if a loved one dies and names you as a beneficiary), a divorce settlement, a year-end job bonus, an income-tax refund, or a wad of cash given for a special occasion. If you've ever come into such a chunk of money, don't blow it. Spend the money wisely by reducing that credit-card debt you've been carrying.

Leverage the Internet to Spend Less

Many of us routinely pay too much for goods and services that we could get for far less, if only we'd take the time to comparison-shop. Thankfully, with the power of the Internet, you can easily cut your spending and apply the savings to your debt by shopping online. Here's what to do: Come up with a list of at least five things you can do to curb your spending. Also think about major categories of spending where you'd like to reduce your costs. Then visit the financial website http://www.lowermybills.com, which helps you to save money in 18 categories of household bills, ranging from home-equity loans to auto insurance to long-distance telephone service. They do the hunting for you to make recommendations about where you could be saving money, but don't rely exclusively on leveraging the Internet. Get creative about your finances. Look at ways you can save money by modifying some of your spending habits, whether it's checking out books from the library or using a movie service like Netflix. Whatever savings you achieve, including things like clipping coupons or canceling unnecessary magazine subscriptions, make sure you apply that "extra" money to your debts.

Sell Stuff You Don't Want, Need, or Use

Are there pants, sweaters, dresses, or suits in your closet that you haven't worn in a month of Sundays? That clothing would be far more valuable in the hands of someone less fortunate than you. Donate unused or unwanted clothing, electronics, and other household goods to charity and get a tax deduction for your generosity. Alternatively, you could have a garage sale and use the proceeds to lessen your credit-card debt.

Turn a Hobby into Cash

Whether you turn a hobby into a cash-making business, sell new or used products online, or stuff envelopes for another business, the key factor is a no-cost or low-cost venture from the privacy of your own home.

Adjust Your Withholdings at Work

If you're getting a big income-tax refund from the government each year, you are squandering a precious financial opportunity. Currently the IRS reports that the typical refund check tops $3,000. For those of you who routinely receive tax refunds, instead of giving the government an interest-free loan get your money now. Go to the HR office at work and adjust your W-4 withholdings so that your employer takes less money out of your paycheck. This way you'll have more money coming in every pay period, and you can use that extra money to knock down your debts. Check out IRS publications 505 and 919 at www.irs.gov to adjust your withholdings so that you don't end up owing taxes.

Get a Second Job

Consider getting a second job or part-time work, even if just for three months. Additional income not only can provide you with money to eliminate credit-card debt but it can also help you to build an emergency savings fund.

Squeeze Money from Your Residence

Whether you rent or own, getting a roommate or housemate is another way to generate income. If you can tolerate having an extra person around, you'll likely find takers willing to lease a spare bedroom in your attic or basement. Taking in a roommate will provide you with extra cash to pay toward your debts. However, before forging ahead if you are a renter, be sure you're not violating any clauses in your rental contract by letting someone else live with you.

Start Using Cash More Frequently

Studies show that shoppers tend to buy more than they had planned, and purchase higher-priced items, when they use credit cards versus cash. Forking over hard-earned dollars makes you think about the value of your purchases. So before you go on a shopping spree, hit the ATM first, armed with your budget, and take out exactly the maximum amount you've determined you can afford. Later, when you are out of cash, accept that your spending spree is over. Resist the temptation to whip out plastic to buy more stuff, and watch your credit rating soar as a result.

Create a Strategy to Lower Your Credit-Utilization Ratios

Now that you know a host of methods to eliminate credit-card debt, I want to turn now to several ways you can strategically lower your credit-card utilization. Let me state right away that it's always best to pay down debt as opposed to shifting it around. However, for most people it's not always possible to pay off instantly all their credit-card debt in its entirety. So what can you do in that case? You can shift debt around in order to lower your rate of using credit cards. Remember that 30% of your FICO® credit score is based on the amount of credit-card debt you're carrying versus the amount of credit you have available. For example, if you have $15,000 in available credit on all your cards and have charged $10,000 on those cards, you've used up two-thirds of your available credit, and your credit-utilization rate is 67%—not good.

To increase your credit scores, it's imperative that you slash your ratios. No one knows the magic number when it comes to credit-utilizations rates; FICO® doesn't reveal the "ideal" percentage. However, we do know that higher credit-utilizations rates generally translate into lower FICO® scores. Statistically speaking, those with lower rates have higher FICO® scores. Therefore, it's best to keep your credit utilization at a maximum or 25% to 35% for an optimal FICO® score. If you maintain zero credit-card debt by paying off your bills in full each month, realize that you may not have a 0% credit-utilization rate because of three factors: the date when you pay your bills; the date when a creditor reports your payment history to the credit bureaus; and the date that your credit report is pulled to generate a credit score.

Besides, you need not worry about having a 0% rate simply because, believe it or not, individuals with a 0% credit-utilization rate actually have lower credit scores—an average of just 678 versus 745 for those with credit-utilization rates of 1% to 10%. Take a look at the chart below from CreditKarma.com based on a random sample of 70,000 credit scores.

Source: CreditKarma.com

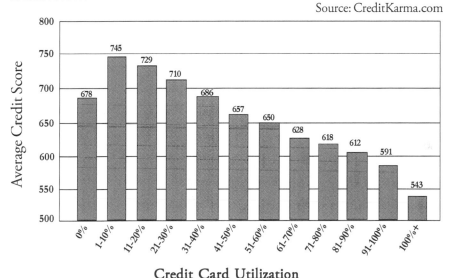

Credit Card Utilization

How is it possible that those with a 0% credit-utilization rate have average credit scores of only 678 points? CreditKarma.com suggests a few likely causes. First, it's possible that individuals with a 0% rate have no credit cards at all. This could actually hurt their credit rating because remember that 10% of your credit score is based on the mix of credit contained in your files. Having a credit card, along with other forms of credit, shows that you can manage various types of credit simultaneously. Another plausible reason for that 0% rate is that those individuals never use their credit cards at all. (Another reason to use your credit cards on occasion is to keep them active.)

If you don't have the money to pay down debt, here are the four chief strategies to lower your credit-card utilization rates.

⇨ **Use a Home-Equity Loan**

Getting a home-equity loan or an equity line of credit can be a smart strategy for a few reasons. First, the interest rate on home-equity loans (currently in the 6% range) is far lower than what you're probably paying on your credit cards (likely in the 15% plus range). In addition, the interest on home-equity loans is tax-deductible up to $100,000; the interest levied on your credit cards is not. Finally, from a credit-scoring standpoint, mortgage debt is treated more favorably than credit-card debt, so converting that consumer debt is likely to impact your FICO® score positively by helping you to reduce your credit-card utilization rates.

If you decide to consider this strategy, I must issue a very serious word of caution: Don't pay off those credit-card bills and put your home at risk with an equity loan if you're just going to run up your charge cards again. The decision to take out a home-equity loan should not be made lightly. I believe that you should only use your home equity to pay off debt under two circumstances:

1)   You got into credit-card debt because of what I call "The Dreaded D's"—downsizing, divorce, death, disability, disease, or some other disaster such as a business failure or lawsuit; and

2) The situation that threw you into debt has now been rectified. For instance, your employer downsized, but you now have another job, or you were diagnosed with a disease but now have bounced back from your medical problems.

If you got into debt for other reasons of your own doing, such as overspending, and if you haven't learned how to get those impulses under control, I urge you to refrain from tapping the equity in your home to pay off credit-card debt. I've heard heartbreaking stories of people who paid off their credit-card debts by converting those obligations into mortgage debt, only to keep spending while not changing their financial habits and ultimately losing their homes in foreclosure. I don't want this to happen to you.

⇨ **Shift Balances from One Card to Another Existing Card**

Shifting debt from one credit card to another is more art than science, but done properly it can boost your credit scores and also save you lots of money, particularly if you're taking debt from one high-interest card and putting it on a lower-interest card. The key here is to minimize the debt you're carrying on a card that has high credit-utilization and transferring that debt onto a card with a zero balance or low balance. For example, if you have two cards, and each has a $5,000 credit limit, but one has $3,000 in charges while the other one has only $500, your current credit-utilization rate is 35% ($3,500 divided by $10,000). You may be able to improve your credit scores, however, if you spread out some of that $3,000 in debt from the first card. By shifting $1,000 of that balance onto the other card, your overall credit-utilization rate will still be 35%. However, the rate for the first card will drop from 60% to 40%. Meanwhile, the second card will have a new credit-utilization ratio of 30%.

⇨ **Open a New Credit-Card Account**

Opening a new credit-card account can lower your overall utilization ratio even if you don't charge anything additional on that new card. Yes, the inquiry will appear on your credit report, and you will likely take a hit on your credit score as a result. Having that additional line of credit, however, can make up for the ding. After all, your credit-utilization ratio comprises 30% of your score while inquiries account for only 10%. Using the same example as above, assume you that have those two credit cards with a total of $10,000 in available credit and $3,500 in charges for a current utilization rate of 35%. If you open a new credit-card account with a $5,000 limit, your overall utilization rate drops to just 23% because you've charged $3,500 and have a grand total of $15,000 in available credit.

⇨ **Secure an Increase in Your Existing Credit-Card Line(s)**

A fourth and final strategy to bolster your credit-utilization rate is to ask existing creditors for an increase in your credit lines. The principle behind this maneuver is the same as that of opening a new credit account. Essentially it boils down to your having more available credit in order to improve your standing in the eyes of the scoring world. Amid the credit crunch it's likely that your current creditors may do a "hard" pull of your reports, or perhaps they won't if they've already been monitoring your credit files. You'll never know until you ask for a credit-line increase. In the process of doing so, you can ask the customer-service representative if it's necessary for them to pull your credit record. That way you'll know whether or not an inquiry will be generated and whether it's worth it for you to use this strategy.

Before you try this option, some more research from CreditKarma.com is worth examining. Credit Karma wanted to see whether there was a correlation between people's credit scores and the credit limits set by banks and other issuers. Sure enough, there is. Credit Karma sampled more than 500,000 credit-card accounts in June 2009 and compared average users' credit limits with their credit scores. The results showed that across all score ranges, ranging from bad credit to great credit, consumers with higher credit scores had higher credit limits. The chart below tells the story.

Current Average Credit Limit

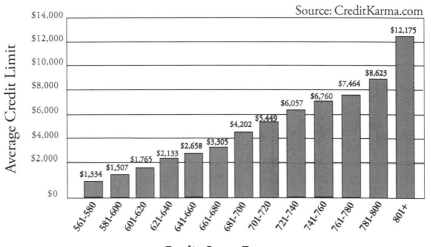

Source: CreditKarma.com

What's more, Credit Karma found striking differences among the credit-card limits set by various companies. Based on its analysis of the top five card issuers, Bank of America had the highest average credit-card limit at $11,288, whereas Capital One had the lowest at $3,524.

What about Student Loans, Car Notes, Mortgages, and Medical Bills?

Until now I've stressed in this chapter that in order to achieve Perfect Credit your focus should be first and foremost on minimizing credit-card debt. That's not to suggest, however, that other forms of debt don't play a role in your credit rating. On the contrary, having a healthy mix of credit, such as a mortgage or auto loan, in your file can bolster your credit profile. On the other hand, installment or mortgage debt can become a problem if you don't pay those obligations, or if all of your bills are so high that you're late in paying any of these debts. Let's look at what you can do about four common scenarios: defaulted student loans, overdue car payments, delinquent mortgages, and past due or excessive medical bills.

How to Fix Defaulted Student Loans

Assume that you used student loans to finance all or part of your higher education. If you took out college loans but did not repay them, that can tremendously damage your credit rating and cause a host of other financial problems. A federal college loan falls into default status if you are supposed to make monthly payments but have not done so for 270 days. For those whose student-loan payments are less frequent, a default occurs once you haven't made payments for 330 days. In either case, the government has the right to take your federal tax refund or garnish up to 15% of your disposable income in order to collect on a defaulted student loan. Private college lenders may also take you to court for that outstanding debt. Defaulted student loans have no statute of limitations, meaning that creditors can hound you for decades, and even snatch your pension money, until your obligation is satisfied. Defaulted student loans will remain on your credit report for seven years.

Fortunately, there are ways to handle defaulted student loans and fix your credit in the process. That's a big help in this tough economy because an increasing number of college graduates (and college dropouts) are falling behind on their loans. According to the Department of Education, federal student-loan defaults were up to 6.9% in 2009, well above their 2008 level of 5.2%. For those carrying private loans, defaults hit 3.37% in 2008 versus 1.47% in 2006 according to Sallie Mae, one of America's largest providers of private loans.

Appealing a Wage Garnishment

The good news is that you can appeal a wage garnishment and request a hearing on the matter to demonstrate why you can't afford the payments or garnishment your lender is seeking. The U.S. Department of Education Debt Collection Services Office (DCS) holds the hearing after you fill out a "Request for Hearing" form regarding your wage garnishment and send it to the Department of Education. You can find the document online at http://www.ed.gov/offices/OSFAP/DCS/forms/ Request.For.Hearing.pdf. Your hearing can be done in person, over the telephone, or in writing. When you submit your "Request for Hearing," make sure that you also send another extremely important document. It is the "Financial Disclosure Statement," a three-page document in which you must document your income and itemize all your expenses. Here is a link to the document online: http://www.ed.gov/offices/OSFAP/DCS/ forms/fs.pdf. The "Financial Disclosure Statement" will be critical in the appeal process and will be closely evaluated, so take the time to list all your bills and provide copies of those bills as requested.

On page 3 of the "Financial Disclosure Statement" you will notice a line that says: "Based on this Statement, I think I can afford to pay $_____per month." This is where you have an opportunity to offer a counter-proposal to the Department of Education about your student loan. Regardless of what you've been asked to pay in the past, you should realistically evaluate your budget and come up with a figure that you can undoubtedly pay (without huge financial strain) month after month. The Department of Education will make a decision about your case within 60 days after your hearing, but in the meantime any wage garnishment that has already started will continue in force.

Four Options to Cure a Defaulted Student Loan

In order to get your student loan(s) out of default, you have four options: consolidate the loan(s); enter a loan-rehabilitation program; pay the loan(s) off completely; or get the loan(s) totally discharged or cancelled. The last two are probably not realistic options. You probably don't have the money to pay off the loan(s), which is why you're in this predicament. Loan cancellations are rare; therefore, you likely will have to "rehabilitate" your loan(s) or consolidate.

Should You Rehabilitate Your Student Loans or Consolidate?

Before you can consolidate, you have to bring your student loan(s) out of default status. You do this by making just three monthly payments on time and in any amount that you and your lender agree upon. To find out if you qualify for loan consolidation, contact the Federal Direct Consolidation Loan Info Center at 800-557-7392 or go online to http://loanconsolidation.ed.gov. If you call, the staff should be able to tell you what your monthly payment will need to be for those three months. One drawback to consolidation is that your credit status remains tarnished. Even though your loan will be paid off and listed as "paid in full" on your credit report, you'll get a new loan through consolidation, and that previous default will remain on your report for seven years. An alternative that will fix your credit and delete negative information from your file is to go through loan rehabilitation.

With rehabilitation you make 9-12 payments—9 for Direct Loans and Federal Family Education Loans or 12 for Perkins Loans—on your student loan(s) in a monthly amount you can afford. In my opinion, this is the preferred route because it will help you to restore credit so that a past default won't haunt you for years to come. For more details check out http://www.ed.gov/offices/OSFAP/DCS/forms/2004.Borrower.Options.pdf. No matter what economic challenges you're facing, you don't have to live with wage garnishments and blemishes on your credit report because of defaulted student loans.

Tips for Paying Off Student Loans Fast

Some of you may be asking, "But what can I do to knock out my student loans more quickly, even if they're not in default?" Fortunately, there are options for you as well. If you follow these seven tips, you'll be rid of your college debt as soon as possible.

1. **Pick the shortest loan-repayment program you can afford**
   If you have federal student loans, you can select from any of four different repayment plans:

   ⇨ **Standard**, which requires you to pay a minimum of $50 per month for as long as ten years;
   ⇨ **Extended**, which also requires at least $50 monthly payments but which lets you pay off your loans over 12-30 years;
   ⇨ **Graduated**, which lasts from 12 to 30 years and allows you to pay as little as $25 a month; and
   ⇨ **Income-contingent**, which permits you to make payments as low as $5 a month and which lasts for 25 years.

   Tip: Don't make the mistake of picking the option that lets you pay the smallest monthly amount. That may help your cash flow in the short term, but in the long run you'll pay thousands more in finance charges. The best strategy is to pay as much as you can possibly afford on your student loans. If you can't swing the standard repayment plan and have to choose a longer plan, then at least pay more than your stipulated minimum. Even if you can add only $25 a month to your regular payment, it will help. Sending in "extra" payments is a short-term financial challenge, but if you bite the bullet now you'll be better off in the long run.

2. **Ask your current or future employer to help you eliminate your student loans**
   A little-known way to get rid of college debts, including both private and federal loans, is to have your employer assist in paying it off. Many organizations will do so if you sign an employment-incentive contract. This means that as a "bonus" or "perk" your job pays your

student loans. In turn, you agree to be a loyal employee and remain with the company for a given time period, say at least two to three years. Getting an employer to pay off your student loans is just another benefit. Companies offer valued employees extra cash all the time, such as hiring/signing bonuses, performance bonuses, year-end bonuses, or holiday gifts. Why are companies willing to offer student-loan assistance? They want to hire and retain top talent.

Tip: The next time you're up for a raise or performance appraisal, raise this subject with your boss. You can also bring up the matter to a prospective employer when you're job-hunting. Just wait until after you have received a firm job offer and started the salary-negotiation phase. By following this advice you may not have to pay your student loans at all.

3. **Get the federal government to pay off up to $60,000 of your college debt**
   The government's Federal Student Loan Repayment Program can be a huge windfall to anyone with federal student loans. Administered by the Office of Personnel Management, this program allows any federal agency that you work for to pay off $10,000 annually of your federal student loans up to a maximum of $60,000. For more information, call 202-606-1800 or visit http://www.opm.gov.

Tip: Here is a link to the specific page on the OPM website that will give you all the information you need to know about the Student Loan Repayment Program: http://www.opm.gov/oca/pay/StudentLoan/. Be sure to check out the "Fact Sheet" and "Questions and Answers" section on the left side of the website.

4. **Get a deferment, forbearance, or loan cancellation during periods of economic hardship**
   Most people think that only students who are enrolled in school can get deferments. Nothing could be further from the truth. Nearly anyone with an economic hardship can qualify for a loan deferment or forbearance, and some people with chronic financial problems may be eligible to get their loans canceled altogether. Sallie Mae, the

nation's biggest student lender, offers deferments for nearly 20 different scenarios. Loan payments can be postponed for the unemployed, for new mothers reentering the workforce, for volunteers at non-profit agencies, for military enlistees, etc. Even having excessive credit-card debt or unusually high personal expenses can get your monthly loan payment lowered. If you've had a string of bad luck—say you went through a divorce, got laid off, then had a car accident—you can qualify. Also, if you've had a protracted hardship such as a medical illness, the Department of Education may cancel your loan indebtedness.

Tip: To claim an economic hardship and reduced student-loan repayments, fill out a simple two-page form called a "Statement of Financial Status." You can find it online at http://www.ed.gov/offices/OSFAP/DCS/forms/fs.pic.pdf. If you have private loans, ask your lender about deferment and forbearance options.

5. **Use volunteer activities or certain work to qualify for loan forgiveness or cancellation**
   A host of working professionals can have their loans forgiven or cancelled. These include police officers, lawyers, teachers, nurses, and doctors. People who volunteer for AmeriCorps, VISTA, or the Peace Corps or who help impoverished people can also have their student loans written off. These loan-cancellation programs are available for the asking.

   Tip: More than two dozen loan-cancellation and loan-forgiveness programs are detailed in my book titled *Zero Debt for College Grads*.

6. **Negotiate loan rates and terms on any new federal student loans**
   Each year, at the beginning of July, Congress adjusts the interest-rate caps charged on federal student loans. However, contrary to popular belief, Congress doesn't "set" the rates for student loans. Instead, the feds impose a maximum interest rate that lenders can charge. Lenders then set their own rates based on what the market will bear. Therefore, if you're willing to negotiate for more favorable rates and loan terms, you can find many lenders who will agree to charge a rate lower than

the federal maximum. Interest rates are currently being reduced for federally subsidized Stafford loans. (With subsidized loans the government pays the interest while the student is in school.) As of this writing, the interest rates on new subsidized Stafford loans were:

⇨ 6.0% for loans first disbursed July 1, 2008 to July 1, 2009
⇨ 5.6% for loans first disbursed July 1, 2009 to July 1, 2010
⇨ 4.5% for loans first disbursed July 1, 2010 to July 1, 2011
⇨ 3.4% for loans first disbursed July 1, 2011 to July 1, 2012

Tip: Ask a lender for lower interest rates based on (a) having payments automatically deducted from your checking/savings account; (b) making a set number of on-time payments; and/or (c) earning good grades.

7. Consolidate student loans carefully

Anyone with student loans receives lots of offers in the mail from lenders seeking to consolidate your loans. If you do consolidate, do so wisely. You'll have to keep your private and federal loans separate; you can't consolidate those two groups. But be careful which loans you roll into one bigger loan. For instance, let's say you took out federal Perkins loans while you were in school. In most cases you wouldn't want to combine Perkins loans with other types. The reason is that Perkins loans have better "loan forgiveness" benefits for people who go into teaching, and you can lose those benefits if you consolidate them.

Tip: For more information visit http://www.loanconsolidation.ed.gov. The major advantage of consolidating student loans is that your monthly payment will be reduced, freeing up some of your cash flow each month. The biggest drawback is that, because consolidated loans are stretched out over a longer repayment period, you'll wind up paying two to three times as much as you would have paid by not consolidating.

Don't Let Your Car Note Drive You Crazy

If you're in over your head with an expensive car note, it's time to think about getting from underneath that burden. Here are some options for dealing with overdue car payments when you're struggling to pay for your vehicle.

⇨ **Get a Payment Extension**

If your financial difficulties are temporary, or if you just hit a brief bad patch, you may be able to convince your auto-finance company to give you a payment extension. Here's how it might work. The auto company would allow you extra time to make a payment without reporting you to the credit bureaus. Alternatively, they could agree to let you forego one or two payments in the short term and then tack on those extra payments to the end of your car contract. Either way, you keep the car, get a bit of breathing room financially, and don't damage your credit rating.

⇨ **Rewrite Your Contract**

As an alternative to getting your car repossessed (which, believe me, auto companies don't want to do), you might inquire about having your contract rewritten. Perhaps they would agree to a longer repayment period, thereby lowering your payments, or in some instances you might qualify for a lower interest rate. This is frankly a long shot, but it's worth pursuing before they take the car or you agree to a "voluntary" repossession, both of which will seriously mar your credit rating.

⇨ **Consider Refinancing Your Auto Loan**

If you try to negotiate with your auto-finance company but can't get them to comply, you might consider refinancing your auto loan with another lender, especially if that will get you a lower interest rate. Many people don't know that you can refinance your car loan, just as you can refinance a mortgage. But car refinancing is easier and faster, and it requires no points, appraisal, or closing costs. To lower your car payments, try Capital One Auto Finance (http://www.capitaloneauto.com), the premier vehicle lender in the United States. Refinancing takes just 15 minutes and saves an average of $1,353 over the life of the loan. What will you do with the money you save? Pay down all those credit-card debts, naturally.

⇨ **Save Money on Car Costs**

In addition to your monthly payment, a lot of other expenses are involved with having a car. To save on gas and parking, park for free on the street or take public transportation. To save on car insurance, opt for a higher deductible in exchange for 10% to 25% off your annual premiums or ask your insurer about discounts for being a good driver, having an alarm system, or completing a defensive-driving course.

Advice to Those with Delinquent Mortgages

If you've tried negotiating with your mortgage lender, have adjusted your budget, and done everything in your power to pay your house note but have still come up short, it may be time to seek government assistance. Part of President Barack Obama's $75 billion mortgage-rescue plan is aimed at helping people avoid foreclosure by either refinancing their house notes or modifying their loans. Many lenders, large and small, are even agreeing to delay foreclosure proceedings for homeowners who meet certain criteria. To find out whether you qualify for assistance under the Home Affordable Modification Plan under President Obama's initiative, visit http://www.MakingHomeAffordable.gov.

Are You Eligible for a Loan Modification or Refinance?

To be eligible for a loan modification, you have to meet five criteria: the home must be your primary residence; you must owe less than $729,750 on the home; you must be having trouble making payments; your mortgage must have been finalized before January 1, 2009; and your total housing payment (principal, interest, taxes, and insurance) must exceed 31% of your gross income. To be eligible for a loan refinance, your existing mortgage must also be owned or insured by Fannie Mae or Freddie Mac. To find out whether your home loan is owned or insured by Fannie or Freddie, contact:

⇨ 1-800-7FANNIE (8:00 a.m. to 8:00 p.m. EST)

⇨ www.fanniemae.com/loanlookup

or

⇨ 1-800-FREDDIE (8:00 a.m. to 8:00 p.m. EST)
⇨ www.freddiemac.com/mymortgage

The Obama administration says that its plan will help as many as 5 million homeowners refinance their mortgages and save their homes. The government's loan-modification program is designed to lower your interest rate to below 5%, perhaps as low as 2%, so that your payment is no more than 31% of your gross income.

⇨ **Get Your Documents in Order**

Once you determine that you're eligible for a loan modification, pull together a slew of paperwork: paycheck stubs, your last tax return, recent mortgage statements, an itemized list of your expenses, as well as anything that substantiates your financial hardship, such as those large medical bills and a letter describing why you fell into trouble in the first place (loss of income, etc.). You'll need all these documents to back up your request for help. Only your current lender can modify the terms of an existing mortgage.

⇨ **Be Prepared for a Slow Process**

Keep in mind that a loan modification is not mandatory. Lenders are doing these adjustments on a "voluntary" basis. Therefore, banks don't have to reply to you within, say, 30 or even 60 days. However, banks are getting "incentive" payments to do loan modifications, so when President Obama launched this rescue plan nearly all the major banks got on board and agreed to postponements and freezes on foreclosures. Many of them signed agreements to participate. You can find a list of lenders/loan servicers involved with the program on the following website: http://www.makinghomeaffordable.gov/contact_servicer.html.

⇨ **Contact a HUD-Approved Housing Counselor**

If you get stonewalled in trying to negotiate directly with your lender or loan servicer, you're not alone. The same thing has happened to millions of people. To minimize your frustration and possibly receive faster help, get a trusted third party involved. Contact a reputable non-profit agency such as the National Foundation for Debt Management (NFDM), whose HUD-approved housing counselors can offer you free assistance. You can reach NFDM at http://www.NFDM.org or 866-409-6336.

What to Know If You Think You Might Go into Foreclosure

The foreclosure crisis is wreaking havoc on millions of Americans. In 2009 there were 2.8 million foreclosure filings in the U.S., according to California-based RealtyTrac, an online marketer of foreclosed homes. RealtyTrac's statistics include all types of foreclosure such as default notices, auction "short sales," and bank repossessions. Although the numbers for 2009 swelled by 21% over 2008 levels, the problem unfortunately isn't going away. Between 3 and 3.5 million foreclosure filings are predicted for 2010. Simply put, too many folks can't afford their homes, and many don't know what to do about it.

Once you live in a home for any amount of time, whether it's a year or a decade, you naturally start to develop some emotional attachment to your house. You can probably recall family celebrations there, major life changes while you lived in the home, or even just things you did to personalize the residence and make it your own. For all these reasons it can be devastating to lose the house you love and worked so hard to obtain. Nevertheless, sometimes a big mortgage payment, in combination with the other bills and curve balls that life throws at you, can simply become too much to bear financially.

When you miss multiple mortgage payments, you become subject to foreclosure proceedings. There are two forms of foreclosure in America: judicial foreclosure and non-judicial foreclosure. Judicial foreclosure, normally used in states where a mortgage is used as the security instrument on a home, is a lengthy process and involves a court lawsuit. Non-judicial foreclosures typically occur in states that use a deed of trust as the security instrument. Non-judicial foreclosure allows a trust to initiate foreclosure without having to go to court. Other types of foreclosure methods exist, but they are far less common. For instance, strict foreclosure allows a lender to foreclose on a house simply by declaring that a borrower has defaulted. Strict foreclosure is permitted in only a few states such as Connecticut, New Hampshire, and Vermont.

The foreclosure process can vary widely from state to state, but the following is a synopsis of what usually occurs in a judicial foreclosure, one in which a lender sues you in order to get a judgment to seize your home and auction it off. After you fall anywhere from three to six months behind on your mortgage, your lender will file a court complaint and also a "Notice of Lis Pendens" with your County Recorder's Office. (Some lenders are more aggressive and want to file official notices as soon as legally permissible in order to cut their losses. Others will first try to do everything possible to avoid commencing foreclosure.) The "Lis Pendens" is official notice that you face foreclosure and that the clock is now ticking to bring your past-due payments current. The lender will seek an entry of judgment or summary judgment from the court, which specifies the entire amount due and establishes a sale date for the property. If your defaulted mortgage isn't brought current, usually another three months will pass before most lenders send you a "Notice of Sale," indicating that a foreclosure date has been set. This notice will be posted on your property and also entered at the County Recorder's Office. Depending on your lender and the state in which you live, foreclosure proceedings can vary, especially with regard to the speed with which your bank acts. No matter what happens, if you face foreclosure, deal with the issue head-on. Don't hide from your lender or keep your fingers crossed in the hope that an eleventh-hour solution will magically appear.

How to Eliminate Pesky Medical Bills

Many people don't realize that doctors are willing to negotiate costs with patients who don't have healthcare coverage. Consumers can also use the strategies below if they have outstanding medical debts or are planning to have a medical procedure but know it won't be covered by insurance.

1. Ask the right person for a discount: This is almost always the doctor herself, not the office manager or secretary at the front desk. Let your doctor know if you're uninsured or your healthcare company won't cover certain procedures. For example, you might say: "Doctor, I really want to have this procedure done, but I'm afraid that I won't be able to afford it since my insurer won't cover the cost. Can you work with me on my bill so I can get the care that I need?"

2. Be flexible and open-minded: Don't make it seem as though you're trying to weasel out of paying. Let the doctor know that you understand her situation too. She's working hard and deserves to be fairly compensated, so indicate flexibility and a willingness to work out a reasonable deal. For example, if a doctor can't offer you a significant price break, you might ask ask: "At the very least can I establish a payment plan with your office to pay this bill over one year or some agreed-upon time frame?"

3. Arm yourself with information: Before having any kind of check-up, exam, surgery, or medical procedure, you should know the going rates for such services. Hospitals often will slash your bill from full price to what they charge Medicare, since that's seen as a benchmark for costs. Look up Medicare reimbursement rates on the Center for Medicare and Medicaid Services website at http://www.cms.hhs.gov. With this knowledge you can ask for a significant price reduction. The same thing applies to old medical bills that are past due. Insurance companies typically pay only one-third to one-half of what they're billed by doctors, hospitals, and clinics. Why should you pay more than insurers pay?

4. Use cash as leverage: If a doctor normally bills $150 for a routine physical, it would not be unreasonable to say: "I believe that your insurance rate for physicals is $150. Is it possible for me to pay $75 if I pay in cash today?" You may not get a whopping 50% off your doctor's bill, but even a 25% or 30% discount would be a welcome price break.

5. Hire a medical advocate: If your own efforts at getting a hospital or healthcare provider to reduce a medical bill prove unsuccessful (perhaps because the hospital is demanding a lump-sum payment), a qualified medical-advocacy agency will likely be able to convince the hospital to accept a payment plan. For help contact Medical Billing Advocates of America (www.billadvocates.com), which has specialists all across the country who help patients deal with health-related bills.

Hopefully by now you have a very solid game plan for tackling your debts, negotiating with creditors, and enhancing your credit rating at the same time. To maximize your scores, you should always strive to pay down credit-card debt first. After that you can strengthen your credit profile by handling other forms of debt wisely so that none of your bills ever become unmanageable.

Chapter 8:
Fix Errors and Protect Your Credit

Consumer groups estimate that 70% of all credit reports have mistakes in them. That's an awful lot of misinformation, and it could be costing you money. If you have errors in your credit file and you're in the market for a loan, you could wind up paying a lot more in interest than you should. Mistakes happen for a lot of reasons. Sometimes there's an inputting error by a clerk who erroneously types your name, and you get confused with someone else. Or maybe one of the digits in your Social Security number is inadvertently transposed. In other cases family members have found that their credit files somehow get mistakenly commingled. Whatever the cause, you should deal with such mistakes in credit reports as soon as you discover them.

Because of the massive amounts of credit information flying around, it's no wonder that mistakes routinely occur. Roughly 100,000 organizations supply information to credit-reporting agencies. These organizations include banks, lenders, collection agencies, credit-card companies, leasing firms, utility companies, and any other entity that extends credit or reports information about you. The average person's credit report is updated five times per day. Five billion pieces of information are added to credit files every month, and two million credit reports are ordered each day from credit bureaus. We already know about dominant players in the credit industry such as Equifax, Experian, and TransUnion, but more than 1,000 consumer-reporting agencies exist in the United States. Clearly, because of sheer volume alone, errors in credit files are bound to happen, but if there's a mistake it's up to you to fix it.

Each credit bureau has a dispute-resolution process that requires you to write a letter indicating what information is inaccurate or incomplete in your credit file. Under the Fair Credit Reporting Act, the bureau has 30 days to investigate your claims and notify you of the results. Writing the credit bureaus is most effective when there is identity confusion, when personal information is listed incorrectly, or when your file contains wrong data such as account that you never opened. But let's say that you find an error based on misinformation supplied by one of your creditors. This would be the case if you closed an account that still shows as being open; if you have been reported as paying late but actually made a payment on time; or if you paid off an account that still shows a balance. In all of these instances it's best to contact the source of the information and ask them to fix the mistake. If it's a legitimate error, without much to dispute, the company should address the problem. Start with the creditor. Errors disputed and resolved at the creditor level are likely to remain off your credit report. Updates to your credit file usually take about 30 to 45 days. If you're in the market for a mortgage, you can have mistakes in your report fixed in 48 hours through a process called "Credit Re-Scoring." This arrangement allows mortgage bankers to submit proof of a mistake in your credit file directly to credit agencies, which then give your file priority status and update your credit information electronically. This way an error in your file doesn't cost you money or jeopardize your chance to get that mortgage.

Tips for Disputing Inaccurate Information with Your Creditors

When you see erroneous payment or status information in your credit file, you should take up that dispute with your individual creditor before contacting the credit bureaus. Examples of the types of erroneous information you should dispute with a creditor are:

⇨ **Wrongfully reported late payments**
Maybe a creditor reported you as being 30 days past due, but you weren't. Or perhaps the severity of your delinquency has been overstated, as would be the case if you were 60 days late paying a bill but reported as being 90 days late.

⇨ **Collection accounts**

If an account in collections contains inaccurate information, contact the creditor to clear up the matter. They may have added additional fees, interest charges, or penalties that caused the outstanding balance to grow enormously. Or perhaps you didn't even realize you had an account in collections due to diverted mail or an address change. Whatever the circumstance, if there is a reason for you to dispute collection-account information, you'll be best served by starting with the creditor.

⇨ **Inaccurately noted account status**

Contact any creditors that have misreported your account status to the credit bureaus. Your account status includes whether your account is open or closed, current or past due, charged off or not, and so on.

⇨ **Account-ownership mistakes**

Are there accounts on your credit report that show as joint obligations but are just debts of your spouse or someone else? Or what about an account for which you're listed as an "authorized user" but are actually a co-signer and joint user? In each of these cases, you should contact the creditors and ask them to amend or update the account-ownership information shown on your report.

⇨ **Negative and erroneous information about your account status**

Any negative payment information or comments about your account that are erroneous should be deleted from your credit reports. For instance, if your report shows "Account Closed By Credit Grantor" but you closed the account, ask the creditor to change it to "Account Closed By Consumer." Or if a creditor has reported inaccurate information about your past credit usage, which appears in the "high balance" field of your report, request that this information be corrected as well.

⇨ **Inaccurate "balance" information**

Since your creditors report your balances to the bureaus every month, it's not uncommon to find that there is some lag time between when you pay your bills and when your creditors get around to notifying

TransUnion, Experian, and Equifax about those payments. So don't be concerned if your "balance" shows $2,200 but you made a payment two weeks ago of $200 and know your correct balance is $2,000. What you should watch out for, however, are major discrepancies in your reported balances. For instance, if your balance was reported as $2,200 but was really $220, ask a creditor to correct its records and your credit reports.

For all of the errors mentioned above, and especially for disputes about payments (i.e., amount paid, account status, allegedly late payment), always start out by going directly to your creditor and requesting that it delete outdated information or update inaccurate information in your report. If a creditor doesn't respond favorably, you'll need to get more aggressive by contacting supervisors, drafting formal letters, and supplying documentation that supports your claims. (For those of you who need to embark on an aggressive campaign, I'll give you strategic advice in Chapter 10 on how to undertake serious negotiations with creditors as well as collection agencies.) For now, though, let's turn to what you can and should dispute directly with the credit bureaus.

Fixing Errors and Correcting Credit Files Directly with the Bureaus

Consumers write to credit bureaus for all manner of help, but unfortunately many of these efforts are misguided. Sometimes people want assistance in improving their credit scores. At other times they may ask the credit bureaus about why an account is showing up negative, as if the bureaus put that information there and not the creditor.

In most instances, though, people write the credit bureaus in order to seek some change in their reports. Although Equifax, Experian, and TransUnion will accept your inquiries and letters, they rely primarily on the information they gather from your creditors such as lenders, credit-card issuers, retail companies, and collection agencies. These entities are also known in the credit world as "furnishers" because they provide information about you to the bureaus. The credit bureaus, in turn, act as data repositories. Updates from creditors or furnishers form the heart of the information that bureaus compile in your credit files. Thus, the credit bureaus will change something only if you submit a formal, written request disputing something in your credit file and if your creditor can't validate its data within 30 days.

Knowing this fact, you can also dispute with the credit bureaus the same information you may already have disputed with your creditors:

* Wrongfully reported late payments
* Inaccurate collection accounts
* Inaccurately noted account status
* Account-ownership mistakes
* Negative and erroneous information about your account status
* Inaccurate "balance" information

Again, it's best to go to the creditors first before disputing the above matters with Equifax, Experian, and TransUnion. That way you creditor may be more likely to validate your dispute as opposed to denying it. It also might reduce the chances of the negative information's being erroneously reinserted into your files by the creditor at a later date. Here is other information you should dispute directly with the credit bureaus:

⇨ **Mistakes concerning public records**
Any inaccurate information concerning public records should be disputed immediately. For example, if an account was supposed to be charged off in a bankruptcy proceeding but is still appearing on your credit reports, file a dispute with Equifax, Experian, and TransUnion. Additionally, if a judgment for $6,300 shows up in your credit file but the judgment was really for $630, dispute that information too. Remember, however, that changing certain public information such as case number, court location, or even judgment amount will not impact your credit score.

⇨ **Accounts that are not yours**
Credit accounts that you are responsible for repaying include those in which you are or were the individual user of the credit, a co-signer, or an authorized user. If accounts appear on your credit report that you don't recognize at all, you should dispute them with the bureaus.

⇨ **Outdated negative information in your files**

If you find outdated negative information that needs to be deleted, write the credit bureau a letter to that effect or use their online dispute service to summarize your dispute. Remember that most negative information must come off your credit report after seven years. Don't dispute positive information that has been on your credit report for more than seven years, such as a closed account that had a good payment record. Even after you pay off or close an account, it stays on your credit report for ten years. That's a good thing because it adds to the length of your credit history and gives you a stronger mix of credit in your files.

⇨ **Errors in the "high balance" amounts shown on your credit-card accounts**

In monitoring my credit files, I have noticed many instances in which my Equifax credit reports contained erroneous data about my credit-card accounts. In particular, certain accounts were shown as having a "high balance" equal to the "limit" on the card. These mistakes probably resulted from coding snafus or entry errors. Recall that your "high balance" is supposed to show the highest balance you've ever charged on a card, whereas the "limit" indicates the maximum amount of credit available to you. Because credit-scoring companies heavily weight your credit utilization by examining your outstanding balances versus the amount of credit you have available, it's imperative that bureaus have the correct balance information on file. Otherwise your scores could be lower than they should be.

⇨ **Errors of omission**

Be on the lookout for information that may have been omitted from your credit reports. For example, a 2009 review of my files revealed that two credit-card accounts I opened in the 1990s showed up on my Experian report but not on my Experian or TransUnion reports. The two accounts have since been closed, so I didn't ask the latter two bureaus to add them to my files. However, you may have unreported accounts with a positive payment history that can bolster your credit standing. If they are older accounts that are still open but unreported, they will add to the length of your credit history, which accounts for 15% of your FICO® credit scores. Also, TransUnion's website notes that it stores information supplied to it by creditors who subscribe to the bureau's services. "Creditors usually report account information to us through computer tapes. New accounts may take four to six months from the opening date to appear on a credit report," according to TransUnion. The company adds, "If you would like a specific creditor to report account information to Trans Union, you may wish to contact them directly. If the creditor is a member of our service, you can request that this creditor voluntarily report the account information to us."

⇨ **Unauthorized or fraudulent inquiries**
If someone did a hard pull of your credit file without your knowledge or consent, you should dispute that inquiry with the credit bureaus. Even though credit inquiries remain on your report for two years, they impact your score for only 12 months. So be especially mindful of inquiries generated within the past year and contest any you did not authorize.

What to Expect from Credit Bureaus

It's best to dispute errors one at a time because contesting several alleged mistakes at once may cause your dispute(s) to be thrown out. By law the credit bureaus can opt not to investigate your claims if they deem them "frivolous" or "irrelevant." This is one reason why many people using certain "credit repair" services find that they don't work as well as intended. When the credit bureaus get whiff of such an agency's involvement, they will sometimes ignore multiple disputes on the grounds that they are "frivolous."
You can dispute mistakes with credit bureaus by mail or telephone, but you'll get the fastest results if you initiate a dispute online. Here are the websites and phone numbers you should use when you contact the bureaus to dispute errors:

http://www.investigate.equifax.com or 888-800-8859
http://www.Experian.com/disputes or 866-200-6020
http://www.Transunion.com/investigate or 800-916-8800

Generally speaking, all three credit bureaus allow you to dispute errors related to the "Ownership" of an account or its "Account Information"/ "Status." For example, when you fill out the dispute-investigation forms mailed by the bureaus or when you file them online, you will be asked to check boxes that specify what information you are contesting.

If you dispute "Ownership" of an account, you will check one of these boxes:

* I have no knowledge of this account.
* This account does not belong to me.
* This is not my account; it belongs to a relative or another person with same/similar name.
* This account belongs to my ex-spouse.
* This is a fraudulent account; account opened by someone who stole my identity.
* Fraudulent charges were made on my account.
* Creditor agreed to remove my liability on this account.
* Corporate account.
* I am no longer liable for this account.
* I did not authorize this inquiry.
* This is a fraudulent inquiry.
* Other.

If you dispute the "Account Information" or "Status" of an item, you will check one of these boxes:

* This account is included in my bankruptcy.
* My credit limit and/or high credit amount is incorrect.
* My account balance is incorrect.
* Please verify date of last payment, date opened, date closed, or date of delinquency.
* Please verify the account descriptions shown on my account.
* I have never paid late.
* This account is closed.
* This account is not closed.
* My account is closed per my request to the creditor.
* This account is paid.

* I have paid this account in full.
* I paid this account before it went to collection or before it was charged off.
* Too old to be on file. Please remove.
* Terms are incorrect.
* Creditor agreed to remove charges and/or fees.
* Creditor agreed to remove this account from my file.
* This account was transferred to another lender.
* I am a victim of a natural or declared disaster.
* I have Active Military Duty status.
* Account is deferred.
* This account is settled.
* Other.

There may be variations in some of the wording, but as of this writing these are all the possible reasons for disputes at Equifax, Experian, and TransUnion.

At Equifax and TransUnion you can choose only from either the "Ownership" category or the "Account Information" category that best describes your dispute. You can not make selections from both categories. Equifax's online dispute system allows you also to add a "Dispute Account Statement." There you can type up to 250 characters to provide additional information in support of your dispute.

At Experian you can enter up to 120 characters about your reason for disputing something in your credit file. Experian alerts consumers that it will send your statement to the creditor. For example, assume you check the reason for your dispute as "I have never paid late." If you then want to explain your position, you might add a statement such as "The creditor said they misapplied my payment" or "I moved, but my creditor acknowledged that they erroneously sent the bill to my old address." Such statements will be sent by Experian to your creditor to help them understand why you are disputing certain reported information. (Under federal law all bureaus are supposed to forward your explanatory statements or supporting information to creditors when you have a dispute, but critics say that the bureaus routinely violate this requirement to cut costs.)

At TransUnion the online dispute service specifies that you can make only one submission that includes all of your requests for investigation or changes of information. If you need to make additional requests after your online dispute, you must call or write the bureau. TransUnion's mail-in form, called a "Request for Investigation," includes a section for you to write in additional comments related to your dispute. See Appendix B for a sample dispute letter you can use with the bureaus.

Remember: In the event of a mistake, the burden is on you to notify the credit agencies about that error. And it's not enough simply to say that something is "incorrect." You have to indicate why certain information is erroneous or outdated. Once you do, your claim will be investigated. In an ideal world inaccurate or outdated information would be removed from your credit reports when you dispute such data and supply independent proof of your claim. However, the world of credit is far from ideal. Perhaps that's why less than 2% of consumers' dispute requests result in a deletion due to error, according to the Consumer Data Industry Association.

I've already explained that Equifax, Experian, and TransUnion rely almost exclusively on information supplied to them by your creditors. Therefore, if a bureau contacts one of your creditors about an alleged mistake and that creditor verifies the information you are disputing, the information will remain on your credit file. The bureaus will then write you a letter (or notify you via email if you've filed an online dispute) apprising you of their decision and letting you know that the information stands. If the information you dispute gets deleted or changed, the bureaus will also notify you and give you an updated, free report as required by law. Either way, whether your report is changed or not, the credit bureaus will also tell you that you have two options if your dispute has not been resolved to your satisfaction:

1) You can add a 100-word Consumer Statement to your credit file; or
2) You can contact the creditor directly regarding the dispute.

You don't want to add a Consumer Statement to your file because, as previously explained, it is completely ineffective in today's credit environment and may be viewed negatively by future credit grantors who will see your files. Also, going to the creditor with whom you have a dispute seriously disadvantages you. The bureaus essentially require that you ask your adversary to serve as both judge and jury in your case. Of course, this doesn't preclude you from going to your creditors and negotiating with them or trying to prove your claim. My point is simply that whenever you are unsatisfied with the results of a credit-bureau investigation, neither of the options they supply gives you much leverage.

Mark Kraynak, an expert on the Fair Credit Reporting Act and an attorney who specializes in consumer law, recommends that you use a file folder to keep track of your credit-report disputes. The folder should contain letters you've sent to credit furnishers and the bureaus, dispute forms, receipts, affidavits, and copies of other relevant documents, all of which you may need in the event that something erroneous pops up again in your credit file. Kraynak operates a website called www.ruinedcredit.net and heads Mark E. Kraynak, P.C., which has offices in Atlanta and Denver.

For those dissatisfied with the results of a credit dispute, you have another option other than the two offered by the bureaus. You can take your complaint to the Federal Trade Commission (FTC), the agency charged with enforcing compliance with the Fair Credit Reporting Act (FCRA). The FTC tracks consumer complaints and looks into possible violations of the FCRA. According to the FTC's website, it enters complaints from the public into "Consumer Sentinel," a secure online database accessible to some 1,500 civil and criminal law-enforcement agencies in America and abroad. While the FTC does not solve individual consumer complaints, all the complaints is does receive are examined to help the agency detect patterns of wrongdoing. This can ultimately lead to investigations and prosecutions for illegal acts. To file a complaint, in English or Spanish, call the FTC at 877-382-4357 or contact its online Complaint Assistant at http://www.ftccomplaintassistant.gov.

Protect Your Credit from Identity Theft

To enhance your credit reputation, you can do more than fix mistakes that may be in your credit files. You should also guard against identity theft, which is the fastest-growing white-collar crime in this country. Identity theft occurs when someone steals your personal information, such as that contained on your Social Security card or driver's license, and then uses that data to make purchases, open accounts, or obtain credit under your name. Unfortunately, identity theft affects up to 10 million Americans each year as crooks get increasingly sophisticated and more determined in their efforts to target new victims. Some identity thieves use online "phishing" scams to get you to divulge private information; others use decidedly low-tech methods such as stealing your wallet or "dumpster diving" to obtain credit-card numbers and other information about you. An identity thief can be a total stranger or a friend. No matter who the identity thieves are or what tactics they use, rest assured that these con artists don't have full run of the house. There are ways you can fight back to protect your identity, maintain your credit rating, and keep your finances intact.

You can use five strategies to deter, detect, or minimize the impact of identity theft:

* Monitor your credit regularly.
* Take preventative safety measures to avoid ID theft.
* Use fraud alerts.
* Initiate a credit freeze.
* Consider buying ID-theft insurance.

The preceding chapter discussed credit monitoring in detail, so the remainder of this chapter will cover the last four strategies.

Take Preventative Safety Measures to Avoid ID Theft

To decrease your chances of falling victim to identity theft, you should shred sensitive documents before discarding them, never carry your Social Security card, and say no to strangers who solicit over the phone or via email asking for personal data.

In addition, don't be careless about leaving your purse or wallet around others, even if they're coworkers, close friends, or family members. Believe it or not, one of the most common places where identity theft occurs is in the home and at work. You may think nothing of letting your handbag sit on your desk at work, but what about visitors to the office, the delivery guy who brings pizza for lunch, the cleaning lady who comes by your desk regularly, and any number of other individuals who have access to your work environment? Lock up your wallet, purse, or handbag. Better safe than sorry.

Another way to protect yourself is to take a cue from the companies you do business with and learn what they're doing to safeguard your personal information. In 2009 the FTC launched a website to help organizations covered by "Red Flag Rules" to design and implement identity-theft prevention programs. Red Flag Rules require a host of businesses and organizations, such as your creditors and financial institutions, to create written programs to identify the warning signs of identity theft, spot those warning signs, and take the proper steps to respond to those warnings. The purpose of Red Flags Rules is to decrease the frequency of identity theft. To learn more, read the publication "Fighting Fraud with the Red Flags Rule: A How-To Guide for Business," which is available at www.ftc.gov/redflagsrule.

Use Fraud Alerts

Fraud alerts and credit freezes help you thwart identity theft by preventing a crook from opening credit in your name. There are two types of fraud alerts, initial and extended. With an initial alert an ID-theft warning statement is placed on the bottom of your credit reports. This statement alerts your creditors that you may have been the victim of fraud or identity theft. In addition, your phone number is listed on your file so that, if anyone pulls your credit, a lender or creditor is supposed to call you first to verify that it's really you. This process helps to stop identity thieves dead in their tracks. Here are the phone numbers you can call 24 hours a day to set up a fraud alert:

Equifax	800-525-6285
Experian	888-397-3742
TransUnion	800-680-7289

You only need to call one of the credit-reporting agencies to request a fraud alert. Once you put an alert on your file at any one of the three bureaus, all of them are notified about it.

An initial fraud alert is good for a 90-day period. It's best used if you suspect someone may have attempted unauthorized use of your credit or Social Security number. Once you put an initial fraud alert on your file, you are entitled to a free copy of your reports. Upon receipt of your files, review them immediately to search for anything that looks amiss. If no fraud is apparent, you can either ask that the alert be dropped or simply allow it to expire in 90 days. If you do detect evidence of identity theft, your next step should be to request an extended alert.

An extended fraud alert lasts for up to seven years and is sometimes referred to as a "victim statement." An extended alert should be added to your credit files if you have been victimized by identity theft, because you'll want to monitor your files closely and safeguard further use of your credit for a long time to come. That extended alert statement will also put potential credit grantors on notice about your situation, requiring them to call you before granting any credit in your name.

Equifax, Experian, and TransUnion all allow you to place fraud alerts on your credit files free of charge. Separately, if you want to submit a credit alert to Innovis, contact that bureau at 800-540-2505 Monday through Friday between the hours of 8:00 a.m. and 8:00 p.m. EST. Innovis does not share its fraud alerts with the other credit bureaus. If you write to the bureaus to place an extended fraud alert, send them a copy of a valid police report and proof of your identity and address. Proof of your identity can be a copy of your Social Security card, a W-2 form, or a pay stub with your Social Security number on it. To confirm your address, send a copy of your driver's license or a recent utility bill or credit-card statement showing your name and residence.

Initiate a Credit Freeze

Credit Freeze laws, sometimes referred to as "Credit Lock" laws, began in California in 2003. All 50 states, in addition to Washington, D.C. and Puerto Rico, now have laws permitting residents to lock or shut down access to their credit reports with the major bureaus. Faced with a credit freeze, an identity thief can't apply for credit in your name because you must first provide a PIN (Personal Identification Number) to the credit bureaus in order to "unfreeze" or "thaw" your credit report and allow access to it.

Surprisingly, few people have locked their credit reports. By some estimates only a few hundred thousand individuals have requested a credit freeze, this despite the millions of people who have been victimized by identity theft. Individuals concerned about privacy and unauthorized access to their credit can also initiate a credit freeze. In fact, many states with such laws have given residents the right to obtain a credit freeze free of charge.

In order to get a credit freeze, you must provide the major bureaus with the following information: a unique PIN, proper identification, and the names of third parties authorized to review your credit file. Equifax does not charge a fee for a credit freeze. It does, however, require that you put your request for a security freeze in writing and send it via certified or overnight mail to Equifax Security Freeze, Post Office Box 105788, Atlanta, GA 30348.

As of July 14, 2009, TransUnion started charging for security freezes. The cost ranges from $3 to $10, depending on where you live. The fees apply only to those who have not been victims of identity theft. To contact TransUnion about a credit freeze, call 888-909-8872 or write to TransUnion Security Freeze, Post Office Box 6790, Fullerton, CA 92834. At Experian you can request a security freeze online at www.experian.com/freeze or submit your request in writing. Experian asks that you send your request via certified or overnight mail to Experian, Post Office Box 9554, Allen, TX 75013.

Unlike the case with initiating a fraud alert, you must place a security freeze with each individual credit bureau. When requesting it, be sure to include your full name, complete address (and any previous addresses if you've lived at your current residence for less than two years), Social Security number, date of birth, and proof of identity/address such as a copy of your driver's license, recent utility bill, or credit-card statement.

Consider Buying ID-Theft Insurance

Considering how widespread identity theft has become, it may be a good idea to purchase identity-theft insurance. A handful of insurance companies nationwide offer this coverage. Since the average victim of identity theft spends about 200 hours and $1,000 to clean up the mess brought on by this heinous crime, identity-theft insurance reimburses you for a range of things such as attorney fees, phone bills, and time lost from your job. Coverage usually goes up to $25,000. As previously noted, some credit-monitoring services also include identity-theft insurance coverage.

Buying any form of insurance is all about the numbers. You're betting that a given peril (such as having a car accident or being victimized by identity theft) may in fact happen to you (although you're hoping that it won't). On the other hand, the insurance company is betting that the danger or peril in question won't happen. Given the odds, however, insurance companies know that in any given year, for any type of insurance, they're going to pay out a certain number of claims. The two big questions are who will file a claim and how much of a payout will that person be seeking. When it comes to identity theft, it's almost a crap shoot regarding that first question.

Anyone can be victims of identity theft. Some famous people who have been targeted include the following:

* Ben Bernanke, chairman of the Federal Reserve Board
* Warren Buffett, billionaire investor and head of Berkshire Hathaway
* Tommy Hilfiger, clothing designer and fashion guru
* J. K. Rowling, author of the Harry Potter book series
* Oprah Winfrey, popular talk-show host and media mogul
* Tiger Woods, professional golf legend

Identity theft is clearly an equal-opportunity hazard. Concerning the second question about how much in claims will be paid out, insurers have a bit more insight. If the numbers on identity theft are to be believed, and current wisdom has it that about 10 million Americans succumb to identity theft each year, the average person has a 3% chance of becoming an identity-theft victim in any given year. So far the odds work in favor of insurance companies. When considered over time, however, the numbers change exponentially. Those 3% odds grow dramatically each year, magnifying the likelihood of being struck by identity theft over a span of, say, 20 or 30 years. In other words, the odds are that you will, at some point, be hit by identity theft. If and when it happens, insurance coverage could prove invaluable.

Hopefully you'll never be crippled by identity theft. If you are a victim, however, act immediately. Alert the credit bureaus so that they can put a notice in your credit files. Also notify your local police department, the FTC (877-ID-THEFT or www.ftc.gov), and the Identity Theft Resource Center (858-693-7935 or www.idtheftresource.org).

Chapter 9:
Enhance Your Credit File Constantly

The experts at Fair Isaac say that paying your bills promptly results in a positive payment record, which is the top factor in calculating your FICO® score. When you keep those accounts open and in good status, you also create a lengthy credit history, another factor in your FICO® score. But there are other ways to improve your credit standing. The first is to add positive information to your file. This can be an especially valuable step for those trying to establish credit, those who've been told they have a "thin" file, or those who may have been denied credit simply because they have no credit file at all.

Let's start with those who have no credit file or score. These scenarios likely result from one of two causes. The first is that you may never have had a traditional credit account such as a car loan or credit card. Another possibility is that you may have had credit recently extended to you but the account is not yet being reported by your creditor. Sometimes it can take as long as four to six months for new accounts to be reported to the major bureaus. In this case it couldn't hurt to contact your creditors to make sure they have reported your accounts.

There's another circumstance, however, in which you should be concerned about having no credit file or score. It's when you have, in fact, opened a credit account but are not showing up in the credit bureaus' records. The likely problem? Somebody probably thinks you're dead. The Social Security Administration supplies something called a "Master Death Index" to credit bureaus, other businesses, and government agencies. If your Social Security number somehow winds up on that list, you are presumed to be deceased. Obviously that makes it pretty tough to get a

Visa card. Even if you have multiple accounts and one of them suddenly includes a death notation, that can literally kill your whole credit file. If you suspect that this has happened to you, contact the Social Security Administration (http://www.ssa.gov) to get help in fixing the problem.

And who fits into the category of having a "thin" credit file? Young adults, immigrants, and women who have not had credit in their own name all fit the classic profile of individuals with "thin" credit files.

So far in this book you've learned how to pull your credit reports, examine them, fix errors, and protect your credit rating. Now it's time to get proactive about what's contained in your credit file. The information that you and others see is based on what creditors have indicated about you, but what about what you have to say? That can and should count for something. If you're smart, you'll augment your credit file to profile yourself in the best possible light. For example, if you notice that a mortgage you paid off appears on one credit report but not on others, you should write to those two agencies and ask them to add that information to your credit file. It doesn't matter that the account is no longer open or has a zero balance. To lenders who view your file it's a significant accomplishment and positive sign. Moreover, having that mortgage shown in your credit file will bolster the "mix," which accounts for 10% of your FICO® score. The idea is to demonstrate that you have a track record of managing a variety of bills and financial obligations responsibly.

Student loans or car loans that were paid off but are not showing up represent another category of positive items you should add to your credit report. These are installment loans that can improve your credit status when properly noted. And lest you think that these traditional loans are automatically listed in your reports, think again.

Plenty of Information Is Missing from Consumers' Credit Files

In the past a number of banks have acknowledged purposely failing to report credit information about some of their customers. The reason is that these financial institutions didn't want certain clients to be poached by the competition's offering a better deal for credit cards or other loans. In fact, the Office of the Comptroller of the Currency once stated, "Some lenders appear to have stopped reporting information about sub-prime borrowers to protect against their best customers being picked off by competitors." Note that the customers in question were "sub-prime borrowers." In other words, the banks weren't worried about customers who had great credit ratings and always paid their bills on time. On the contrary, the banks were neglecting to supply credit information for customers with less than perfect credit ratings, knowing full well that they can be sought-after clients too because lenders can charge them higher interest rates and thus make a lot more money off those individuals.

Some Small Institutions May Not Report Loan Accounts

Certain other organizations may not report loan information, and it has nothing to do with ill intent or profit motives. In some cases a failure to report your loan data may have been a mere oversight. At other times it can be the case that a smaller institution or perhaps a credit union simply does not make a routine practice of reporting consumer data to Equifax, Experian, and TransUnion. The same may be true of local retailers, gasoline companies, and issuers of travel- and entertainment-based credit cards. After all, creditors are not required by law to provide information to the credit bureaus.

If you find that any loan account you have is not showing up on your credit reports, you can send information about your account activity to the credit bureaus and request that it be documented in your files. The big hurdle you may face, though, is that entities that furnish information to the major credit bureaus are required to meet specific provisions of the Fair Credit Reporting Act. One of those requirements is that credit furnishers regularly provide credit updates to the bureaus via automated reporting systems maintained by Equifax, Experian, and TransUnion.

Even if you have a creditor who can't or won't regularly update the bureaus' records, knowing the law can work in your favor. Section 202.6 (b)(6) of the Equal Credit Opportunity Act gives you the right to provide all of your recurring monthly payments as proof of your creditworthiness. By law this information must be taken into account by a lender when you apply for credit, provided that the information is available for that lender's review. So keep good records of any regular accounts on which you are consistently paying and establishing a positive payment record. Think of the process of adding positive information to your credit files as being like tending a garden. In this case the garden is your credit rating, and you want it to flourish. So not only do you have to do the occasional weeding, getting rid of errors or outdated information, but you also have to make sure that the roots of your credit foundation are properly nourished. Just as you would water or fertilize your backyard garden, so too do you want to add a sprinkling of positive payment data or a heavy dose of information related to your responsible use of credit.

It is instructive to know what the credit bureaus have to say about adding positive information to your files. In one of its online FAQ sections, TransUnion notes the following: "Creditors usually report account information to us through computer tapes. New accounts may take four to six months from the opening date to appear on a credit report. We do not add checking or savings account information to our computer files." The agency goes on to state: "If you would like a specific creditor to report account information to TransUnion, you may wish to contact them directly. If the creditor is a member of our service, you can request that this creditor voluntarily report the account information to us."

Positive Information or Improvements Can Boost Credit Scores

What else can you do to add positive information to your file? If you see that your home address is listed incorrectly or that your job of ten years is omitted, that too is something you should have added to the report. Although your address and job information aren't taken into consideration for purposes of computing a FICO® credit score, most creditors and lenders will look carefully at that information to determine how stable you are and therefore how much of a financial risk you may be.

Each of the three primary credit bureaus makes it easy for you to update this type of personal information online, and in many cases the updates will be handled electronically the same day. For example, in 2009 I was able quickly to add information about my current and past employment to my TransUnion report. Ditto for address updates and corrections I made to my Experian file. Some personal information will have to be mailed because the bureaus may need to verify your identity or address. However, information that does not need to be validated by a third party can be processed very quickly.

Last but not least, it is vital to recognize that any incomplete credit report can be harmful to you because it fails to tell the whole story. For example, assume that you had some negative information in your credit file, perhaps a public record such as a bankruptcy or lawsuit. If your bankruptcy or lawsuit is dismissed, that new information should be added to give a true and complete accounting of your credit record. Perhaps that's why Fair Isaac, creator of the FICO® score, tells consumers that updates or improvements to your credit status often have the benefit of increasing your score.

Chapter 10:
Contact Creditors and Negotiate

In the effort to increase your credit rating, you potentially will have to deal with three types of creditors. First are your existing creditors, such as the banks or retailers whose credit cards are in your wallet. The next group of creditors includes collection agencies or lawyers hired to collect a debt. The final category is known as "zombie" debt collectors. These are individuals or companies that may now own your debt, or claim to, even when a debt is many years old. To be effective in dealing with each group, you'll need to adopt a range of negotiating strategies best suited for each scenario. Let's start with how you should deal with your existing creditors.

Tips for Negotiating with Creditors

Many people deep in debt may feel powerless to change their situation in terms of getting creditors to give them a break. Consumers often view credit-card companies as big, impersonal institutions that aren't willing to budge to help people in financial trouble. While it's true that lenders and credit-card issuers are in business to make money, another truth is that companies are run by individuals. Armed with the proper knowledge, perspective, and strategy, you can get a lot of help from the right individuals at these institutions.

Don't make the mistake of thinking that just because you owe money you don't have any power when it comes to dealing with credit-card companies. The truth of the matter is that you probably have far more leverage than you realize. If you've been making payments on time, a credit-card issuer does not want to lose your business, even if you've been making only minimum payments. Thus, if you call and say that you have a better offer (or can get one) from another financial institution, they will probably lower your interest rate on the spot or at least put your account under consideration for a rate reduction if you pay on time for, say, six months straight. They know that it's a competitive market and that consumers get deluged with credit-card and balance-transfer options week after week. It's well worth it for a credit grantor to consider lowering your interest rate rather than to lose your business altogether.

Getting Creditors to Work with You

Probably the most productive thing you can do to get your existing creditors to work with you is to *initiate the process*. As painful as the prospect might seem, you must *call them* instead of the other way around. I know that some of you have gotten used to ducking telephone calls from banks and department stores, asking your kids or family members to say you aren't home, but beginning today you have to be proactive about knocking out your debts. It all starts with your figuring out a workable plan, one that works for the creditor but also you.

Be frank about your situation. If you have recently lost your job, gone through a divorce, gotten sick, or been unable to work, let your creditors know about it. Again, part of your strategy (yes, it's a strategy, but you only want to say what is true) is to appeal to that person's sense of fairness and compassion. After all, you are dealing with another human being, even though some people who've been browbeaten by debt collectors might argue otherwise.

I realize that it's not always realistic to rely on someone else's willingness to help you out of a bind. In fact, I've heard horror stories about consumers who tried to work out financial arrangements only to be berated by debt collectors who used foul language and clearly had no compassion whatsoever. I'm not talking here about dealing with collection agencies, which are quite a different story as I'll discuss later in this chapter. For now I'm referring only to your negotiations with such creditors as the bank or retailer that issues your Visa, MasterCard or Sears card.

Six Things to Ask Your Creditors

Here are the main objectives when you call a creditor about your account. Depending on your circumstances, you want the person on the other end of the phone to do any or all of the following:

* Lower your interest rate.
* Stop late fees.
* Eliminate over-the-limit charges.
* Upgrade your account to "current" status.
* Remove a negative entry from your credit file.
* Accept a partial payment in lieu of the total due without harming your credit.

What's the Best Time to Negotiate with Current Creditors?

It's almost always better to deal with current creditors *before* you actually miss a payment. Creditors are much more willing to work with you if you've paid your bills on time. They're trusting that you'll continue to honor your obligations, even if it means paying only minimum payments or even less than the minimums.

If your credit is already shot, however, it's often more advantageous to negotiate with creditors after the debt you owe is so old that the creditor has perhaps forgotten about it. What do I mean by this? Let's look at the two following scenarios.

Say you lose your job unexpectedly. Statistics indicate that it's not easy to find a replacement job. On average it will take about one month to replace every $10,000 in lost income. Thus, if you were among the top 1% of wage-earners in this country and had a job paying $100,000 or more, it will probably take you about ten months to find a commensurate job. Likewise, if you were earning $40,000 a year, it will take you an average of four months to find a comparable position. In the meantime, if you don't think you can pay all your bills, start calling your creditors immediately. Ask them to lower your interest rate, even if only temporarily. Again, credit-card companies and other lenders are much more willing to be flexible for people who take the time to initiate the process of working out a payment plan or reduced interest deal.

Let's hypothesize, however, that you have an old debt, say a $2,000 bill that you racked up three years ago at a department store. For whatever reason you never paid that bill, and the store has already reported your non-payment. The store has also written off your account as a "bad-debt expense." If you come along now and offer to make a lump-sum payment as a settlement in lieu of payment in full, chances are that the creditor will go for the proposal. After all, that company would rather get some money from you than no money at all. If you work out one of these deals, however, make sure you get the creditor first to agree in writing that it will *completely delete* the negative history from your credit report if you send in the agreed-upon payment.

If a creditor simply marks your past-due account as "Paid" or "Paid as Agreed," that may do absolutely nothing for your credit score. Such creditors also have to agree to delete any references to late payments that they may have previously put on your credit report. Never let them "upgrade" your account status to "Paid Collection" or "Paid Charge-Off." Negative information can stay in your credit file for seven years based on the date of "last activity." So changing your account to "Paid Charge-Off" restarts the clock, adding another seven-year negative mark to your file. Consult Appendix B for a sample settlement letter to get creditors to agree to a settlement and remove negative marks from your credit file.

Negotiating Strategies to Use with Existing Creditors

If you find yourself calling creditors to negotiate the terms of your credit cards, the following are some time-tested strategies you should use.

⇨ **Call in the morning**
Don't call at the end of the day when customer-service representatives are probably tired of dealing all day with irate cardholders. Also avoid calling on the weekends when a supervisor may not be there if you need one.

⇨ **Be polite in making requests**
Get the conversation off to a good start by using good manners. Say "Hello" or "Good morning" to the person you're talking to and call her by name, as in "Good morning, Susan. This is Kim Jones. I'm

calling about my account." Make sure that you sound as though you are making requests, not demands. Be friendly and conversational, not adversarial, to establish good rapport.

⇨ **Request to speak to a supervisor if necessary**
If you get nowhere with the person you're talking to, don't be afraid to "escalate" your call by asking to speak with a supervisor. Even if the conversation isn't confrontational or adversarial, you may require a manager because some employees will admit that they don't have the power to honor your request.

⇨ **Point out your length of time as a customer**
For those of you who've been with a credit-card company for a number of years, use your long-term status as leverage in asking for what you want. This can work in your favor because most banks value loyal, long-term customers and don't want to lose them.

⇨ **Emphasize how much business you've done**
Many of you might have racked up a lot of charges over time. If you've been a valued customer by virtue of having charged many goods and services, make that fact known. Also state that you value the relationship with your creditor and would like to remain a customer in good standing.

⇨ **Stress your willingness pay what you owe**
Creditors may not be inclined to be flexible with individuals whom they perceive as trying to "get one over" on them. The worst thing you can do is to convey the impression that you're a "deadbeat" who is out to avoid paying your obligations. A better strategy is to stress that you are willing to pay your incurred bills.

⇨ **Reveal any extenuating circumstances**
When there have been out-of-the-ordinary circumstances, let your creditors know what they are. For instance, if you lost your job or suffered a major reversal that caused you to miss a payment, tell them. Also make clear whether something occurred that prevented you from receiving bills. Creditors may be willing to waive late fees in such cases.

⇨ **Refer directly to your credit report**

Don't be ashamed to say that a negative mark could hurt your credit report, especially if you're in the market for a new car or house. Describe your situation and say something like the following: "I'd hate for this one blemish from your company to damage my credit standing or my ability to get a loan." Only do this with original creditors; don't try the strategy with collection agents. That's giving them too much information, and they'll turn it against you.

⇨ **Make "first-time" cases work in your favor**

If you've never been late before or had an over-the limit fee assessed, ask directly for removal of a late fee or over-the-limit charge. A little-known fact is that most credit-card companies give their employees the authority (without a supervisor's approval) to waive late fees once every 12 months. Consequently, ask to get those fees annulled. You might be surprised at how easily they will agree.

⇨ **Mention their competition**

As a last resort, when you're negotiating for a lower interest rate, mention that you might take your business elsewhere. The point here is not to make an idle threat, and I wouldn't start the conversation off by suggesting that you might possibly gravitate to a competitor. Nonetheless, you'd certainly be justified in exploring your options and in telling the creditor about other companies' deals if it won't budge on high-interest cards.

⇨ **Document all conversations in writing**

In the event that you have to go back and get something corrected or removed, it helps your case if you can refer to your written notes and say, "I spoke to XYZ person on this date and was told such and such."

⇨ **Initiate requests immediately**

When you want an issue resolved, contact your creditor immediately. Don't wait a couple weeks or more to ask for a rate reduction or a removal of late fees. That lag works against you because it seems as though you didn't care enough about the situation to take action. It also reflects well on you when you initiate the call regarding late payments, as opposed to waiting until they have to contact you.

⇨ **Explain online payment discrepancies**

If you were paying a bill online and for some reason a payment didn't go through, that could be a legitimate reason for the removal of late fees. Another possibility is that, say, you were making minimum payments on a credit card that had a teaser rate of 0% interest for six months. Assume you were paying $100 a month on that card via automatic online payments. Six months later your teaser rate expired, and the normal 14.9% rate kicked in. All of a sudden your new minimum payment might be $115 a month. If you weren't keeping up with things, you would still be automatically sending in $100 payments online. The first time that happened you'd likely get dinged with a late charge for being $15 short in your payment. If you call the credit-card company and point this out, it likely will waive the late fee.

Has Your Credit-Card Limit Been Lowered or Any Accounts Closed?

One area to negotiate with creditors involves closed accounts or reduced credit lines. FICO® research offers some valuable insights into the extent to which banks and other credit issuers have closed accounts and slashed limits during the credit crunch. According to FICO®, from October 2008 to April 2009 about one in five consumers or 33 million U.S. cardholders had credit lines reduced. In addition, 25 million cardholders suffered credit-limit decreases between April and October 2008. The average reduction in credit was $5,100. In summarizing the data, Mark Greene, CEO of FICO®, said: "Our study suggests that lenders are using a scalpel and not a hatchet to trim their revolving credit exposure."

That assessment probably doesn't sit well with consumers, especially those who did nothing to cause their credit lines to be cut. Although 9 million of those 33 million who had their credit limits reduced did have negative information in their files, the vast majority had no such deleterious factors.

If your credit line has been cut or your account closed, don't hesitate to contact your credit-card issuers if you think their actions were unjustified. Although banks are engaging in wholesale culling of their customer ranks for risk-protection reasons, nothing prevents you from calling a credit grantor and asking for a review of your credit history. If you have an on-time payment record, say so. If you have recently paid down credit-card balances, indicate that fact too. To decrease your chances of being hit with a notice from your bank, follow these steps:

* Use your credit card regularly, if not monthly at least once every few months.
* Maintain relatively low balances or pay credit cards off each month.
* Avoid going over your credit limit.
* Pay all bills ahead of their due dates.
* Be mindful of managing other finances well (i.e., don't bounce checks).
* Resist the urge to take big or frequent cash advances on your credit cards.

Using these strategies does not guarantee that creditors won't close your credit-card accounts or lower your limits, but it will limit the likelihood that you will be singled out for such action. In the event that you do get a notice of a change to your credit cards, perhaps because a bank is implementing mass changes for all its card holders, you will be in a better position to ask for an exception.

How to Deal with Collection Agencies

You should also negotiate when it comes to seriously delinquent accounts, like those involving collections or public records. A crucial step in achieving Perfect Credit involves getting bill collectors to work with you when you've had past financial problems. You can greatly enhance your credit standing if you get late payments and other blemishes deleted from your credit file. The way to do this is to call up your creditors and negotiate. Ironically, when your account is past due, that's the best time to negotiate with collection agencies. You have something that bill collectors want—cash. They also have something you want—the power to update your credit report. So your strategy, in a nutshell, should be to dangle the cash carrot before their eyes.

Depending on your account's status (open, closed, charged-off, etc.) and how far behind you are in payments, your goal should be to bring your account current, to set up a payment plan, and/or to agree on a reduced amount the company will accept in lieu of full payment. In all these cases what you're really doing is to settle your account and restore it to good standing. In exchange for that, you must insist on getting the bill collector's agreement to delete negative information that was previously reported about you. At the very least he or she should update your records to reflect a current status of "Paid." However, collection agents will often do this but keep in your credit file such notations as "60 days late." Therefore, negotiate firmly for the elimination of all negative information in your credit report. When you reach an agreement, put it in writing and have both sides sign the pact before you pay a dime. That way you're protecting yourself if the person you're negotiating with reneges on the deal. Don't ever agree to send a postdated or blank check to bill collectors, for you would be giving too much personal information by supplying your checking-account number and bank name.

If you can't pay a debt, bill collectors may be willing to settle out of court for a lump-sum payment of less than the amount you owe or a monthly payment plan, but they also will not hesitate to sue you for the full amount you owe if they feel the debt is large enough to go through the hassle, time, and expense of going to court. So what should you do if you receive a summons and complaint from a creditor? In a nutshell, answer it.

What Happens If You Do Not Answer a Complaint?

If you choose not to answer the complaint, a court will enter a judgment against you, determining that you owe the collector whatever amount was stipulated. You may even be told to pay attorney fees. The collector can then use that judgment to garnish your wages, take money from non-exempt bank accounts, or put a lien on your property.

If you answer the complaint (you usually have about 20 days to respond to the plaintiff's claims), you preserve your right to be able to argue your position in court. You also will be notified of any future court dates. You can use your time in court to state why you don't owe the money the plaintiff claims.

What If You Owe the Money They Claim?

Even if you don't know for sure that you owe the exact amount the debtor claims, you can still use your time in court to stipulate an alternative amount you can afford to pay. The debtor does not want to appear in court any more than you do. He simply wants to get paid. Once the debtor sees how time-consuming this process may become, he may be more willing to enter into a settlement agreement with you.

What If You Don't Have the Money to Pay?

It doesn't matter whether you don't have the money. The debtor can still sue, and the court can still enter a judgment against you. Being broke is not an excusable reason to back out of your financial responsibilities. The court will probably require you to file a financial statement and affidavit concerning your finances. If you can show that you don't have the funds to pay, or that you lack a steady income, the collection agency may be more willing to negotiate a settlement plan. A creditor or collection agency is more likely to reject such a plan if it believes you have the means to pay, knows you have wages that can be garnished, or is aware of property to which a lien can be attached. It is often in the creditor's financial interest, however, if a settlement plan can be negotiated.

Once an account has been charged off or deemed uncollectible, you may be in a better position to negotiate a lump-sum payment to settle your debt. You might try offering 25% or so of the balance you owe. Be careful about offering a monthly payment plan, because if you miss a payment the clock starts over again for the full amount of debt you owe, and negative information could be on your credit report for another seven years.

What to Do When You Get a Summons or Have to Go to Court

Creditors can sell your debt. When they do, collection agencies will often try to threaten you with court action in order to get you to pay a debt. Technically it is illegal for collectors to threaten court action if they do not intend to carry through with it. Taking you to court is time-consuming and expensive for them, and there is no guarantee of a desired outcome.

Typically, then, a court action is a tactic to get you to fork over money or to obtain a default judgment against you if you don't respond to a summons. If you do get a complaint, follow these steps.

1) **Answer it.** If a creditor serves you with a summons or complaint, not merely a letter alleging debt, you must respond within 10 to 30 days as stipulated by state law in order to avoid a default judgment.

2) **Know the statute of limitations.** Creditors have a time limit for obtaining a judgment against you for money you may owe. That statute of limitations varies by state and type of debt. Typically it is anywhere from three to ten years. Creditors can use the limitations in your state or the state where they are located. Often they will use the state with the longer statute of limitations. To check the statute of limitations on debts in your state, contact your State Attorney General's Office or go to www.naag.org and click "The Attorneys General."

3) **Realize that credit bureaus' limits are not the same as statutes of limitation.** Federal law typically requires credit bureaus to drop negative information after seven years pursuant to the date of your first missed payment. (There are exceptions. For example, bankruptcies can stay on for ten years, and tax liens for even longer.) If you live in a state with a three-year statute of limitations on the legal collection of debt, it will still show up on your credit report. If you live in a state that allows judgments to be entered for ten years, it is possible that the debt came off your credit report after six years. So do not use your report to determine whether you owe debt. You *can* use it, however, to verify when the creditor first considered you delinquent in repayment.

4) **Understand that the statute of limitations can start over.** Please note that, if you enter into a payment agreement, you will restart the statute of limitations dating back to day one.

5) **Show up in court.** If you are sued, be sure to appear in court. If you don't, the court can issue a judgment against you for the full amount

the creditor requests. Even if you have reached a settlement agreement prior to court, don't trust the debtor to notify the court that it has been settled. Appear in court, and let the judge or trustee tell you to go home.

Other Important Facts to Know about Judgments and Garnishments

I once had a Facebook friend who wrote me after facing threats from a creditor/bill collector. Because she was out of work, she wanted to know what a creditor can do when you don't have any money. Specifically she wanted to know whether a creditor can sue, get a judgment, and garnish her unemployment checks. The short answer I told her was that, yes, a creditor can sue and maybe even get a judgment. However, her unemployment check was "untouchable" and couldn't be garnished.

Under federal law certain income cannot be garnished. This includes Social Security, retirement-plan benefits, and public assistance or welfare compensation. In addition, unless someone gets a judgment against you for child or spousal support, worker's compensation and disability benefits also cannot be garnished. Unemployment benefits are often exempt as well, but that depends on state law. So if you ever face the threat of a wage garnishment or other type of income attachment, you have to know what is considered an "exempt" asset in the state where you reside. Either way, don't let collection agents or others make idle threats or scare you into paying something you don't owe simply because they claim they are going to confiscate money of yours that is legally protected.

Collection agents and others can garnish vehicles, wages, and bank accounts. When it comes to money in bank accounts, though, if it derives from "untouchable" sources listed above such as Social Security or disability, it is immune to garnishment.

How to Handle "Zombie" Debt Collectors

Consumers often pay off debt for which creditors can no longer seek legal action because the statute of limitations has expired. Consumers sometimes pay off these accounts because they don't know their rights. There are even cases of "Zombie debt" where agencies are collecting on a debt from years ago that one already may have paid off or possibly never have owed in the first place.

Beware of calls from Zombie debt collectors who try to get you to pay on debts that allegedly were incurred 10, 15, or even 20 years ago. In 2009, for example, I received a phone call from such a collector representing National Action Financial Services, which claimed I owed money on a department-store credit card opened in 1988. They said that the bill was last paid in 1989. I told them that I definitely did NOT owe money on the account and that, even if I did, the statute of limitations had long since expired. Can you believe they had the audacity to claim I owed money on a credit card from 20 YEARS AGO? Needless to say, I was not going to stand for this. At first two different representatives from the company literally hung up the phone on me when I told them that I was a financial expert who knew my legal rights and that they should not be trying to scare people into paying alleged old debts. Finally, after I called them a third time, I told a "Mr. Johnson" that if they didn't take my name off their list, or if they called me ever again, I would be reporting them to the authorities. He replied, "I understand. We've already removed your name."

Under federal law any bill collector who sues you or even threatens to sue you after the statute of limitations has expired on a debt is in violation of the Fair Debt Collection Practices Act. So don't be bullied by zombie debt collectors who try to intimidate you into paying debts you may not even have incurred and don't have any legal obligation to pay if the statute of limitations has expired. Each state has different statutes of limitations for past-due debt depending on whether it was based on a written contract, oral contract, promissory note, or open account. Credit cards are usually categorized as open accounts. The statute of limitations for credit-card debt ranges from three to ten years depending on where you live. Again, to check the statute of limitations on debts in your area, contact your State Attorney General's Office or go to www.naag.org and click on "The Attorneys General."

Chapter 11:
Take Time to Educate Yourself

In your quest to achieve and maintain Perfect Credit, it's imperative that you occasionally reassess your use of credit and that you educate yourself about issues affecting your overall finances. There are at least four areas concerning which you should take the time to educate yourself:

⇨ the terms of your existing credit obligations;
⇨ the nature and terms of financial products, services, and credit-related offerings marketed specifically to you;
⇨ the ever-changing world of credit scoring; and
⇨ the credit and debt laws that impact the public.

Notice that the first two areas focus on credit matters unique to you, whereas the final two concern credit topics of importance to all consumers. What happens in those latter two arenas may or may not affect you immediately, but they will have ramifications for your financial dealings. Don't be lax, therefore, about these issues. Chances are good that they will affect you in the future.

Do You Know the Terms of Your Existing Credit Obligations?

Take a moment to consider all the financial obligations you currently have: the mortgage you owe, a car note you may have, that loan you co-signed for a relative, perhaps the student loans you're still trying to eliminate, and yes, of course, those credit cards bulging in your wallet. Do you understand your repayment terms and conditions, the interest rates you're paying, and what recourse you (or your creditors) have if you can't pay as agreed? If you don't know these basics, you're putting yourself at a serious financial disadvantage and jeopardizing your chances of having Perfect Credit.

If you are at all in the dark about the terms of your existing debts, I urge you to become familiar with those obligations. Millions of people don't understand many facets of their debt load simply because they've not had proper financial education. A survey by Capital One highlights consumers' lack of knowledge about their credit cards. Here are some findings of that survey:

⇨ More than 40% of credit-card holders in the U.S. don't know the interest rate on the main card they use.

⇨ More than 50% don't know the fees they would be charged for making a late payment.

⇨ Some 20% of those surveyed did not know their accounts' credit limit.

⇨ Approximately 33% of credit-card holders haven't read the fine print concerning their credit cards. More than half tried but gave up because they couldn't make heads or tails out of the information.

⇨ More than 95% don't know what a "Schumer Box" is. (The 1988 Truth in Lending Act mandated that credit-card offers disclose such information as APR, minimum finance charge, grace period, and late-payment fees.)

The bottom line is that you shouldn't be in the dark about the credit cards and other loan obligations that you routinely pay and that greatly impact your credit rating. Here are ten easy tips to help you better understand your credit-card and loan agreements:

⇨ Always take the time to read the fine print.

⇨ If you don't understand something, call the credit-card company or lender and ask for a "plain English" explanation.

⇨ Use online services and tools such as Bankrate.com to shop for the best credit-card deals.

⇨ Put your credit-card offers side by side so that you can look at the Schumer Box on each and do an apples-to-apples comparison.

⇨ Pull out all your credit-card statements and check the APR and basic terms on each.

⇨ Don't accept a credit-card offer based solely on the interest rate because it could have other terms or drawbacks that make it less attractive.

⇨ Find out the grace period, fees, and minimum finance charges for each card.

⇨ Check your account statements to determine the clauses and provisions pertaining to potential changes in your interest rates or terms.

⇨ Let your government representatives know that you'd like to see better disclosure from credit-card companies.

⇨ Be a proactive consumer by writing to your credit-card companies and letting them know that you want them to highlight key features of their offers and make the fine print easier to understand.

Evaluating Competing Financial Products, Services, and Credit-Related Offerings

It's unfortunate that many consumers don't shop around for the credit cards or other financial products that best fit their needs. More than four out of ten Americans simply accept the cards offered to them without doing any comparison shopping, according to the Capital One survey mentioned above. That's a poor approach to credit and debt management because with just ten minutes of online research, using a service such as CardRatings.com, you possibly can get a much better deal than the one initially offered.

If you're like most consumers, you often get mail, online ads, or telephone solicitations for a host of financial and credit-related products. Most often you probably toss those offers, hit the delete button, or say "No thanks" to those callers. On occasion, however, you may be interested in an offer that comes your way. When you are in the market for financial products and services, it behooves you to spend an appropriate amount of time investigating them. These offers might include any of the following:

⇨ Mortgages (for a first or second home purchase, refinance, or line of credit)

⇨ Installment loans (including auto loans and student loans)

⇨ Insurance (for your home, property, or car)

⇨ Credit services (such as identity-theft protection or credit monitoring)

⇨ Credit-card deals (new card offers, balance transfers, or blank checks)

Depending on the offer you accept, what you think might be a big bonanza may turn out to be a disaster. For example, in its 2009 Credit Card Survey, Consumer Action warned that just because a credit-card issuer dangles a 0% balance-transfer deal before you doesn't mean it's free. Such offers usually impose a fee of around 3%, which equates to $30 on every $1,000 you transfer. Ditto for cash advances on those blank checks that might come in the mail. They too typically carry a 3% fee, and in some cases cash-advance fees run as high as 5%, according to Consumer Action. Again, take your time and proceed carefully. Resist the lure of easy or "fast" money and find out the true cost—in dollars and percentages—for any offer. Ask about interest rates and accrual periods because with certain offers the interest starts accruing immediately on charges or advances. Also keep an eye on fees, which can run the gamut. Annual fees are making a comeback, with many banks charging $20 to $30 for granting you a card. Higher-end and travel-related cards can come with hefty annual fees of $150 to $400. Meanwhile many issuers also assess "account management fees" or "foreign transaction fees" of 1% to 3% for purchases made abroad.

This process of evaluating new credit offers is best done by scrutinizing the terms of your current cards and loans alongside those of the new offers. For instance, have any of your interest rates changed while you weren't paying attention? If they've been ratcheted up through no fault of your own, you'll want to call up your creditors and negotiate for a lower rate rather than accept the first new credit-card offer that comes your way. In other cases you may find that your credit-card company is implementing a change with which you don't agree. It could be a modification of the financial terms, or perhaps the company has notified you about their plans to sell or rent customers' names to their marketing affiliates. If you object, you should write to voice your displeasure. It may be that you have to pay the card off or switch accounts to avoid being subjected to terms you find onerous.

Have Your Needs Changed, and What about Credit Insurance Offers?

Just because you have a certain mortgage, line of credit, or credit card today doesn't always mean that it will be the right product for you forever. Your needs may change, and perhaps, for example, you no longer need a personal line of credit. The idea is to make sure that you current credit products and services adequately meet your needs. In assessing your needs, don't think exclusively about the here and now. Be forward-thinking and make sure you have the appropriate credit (or even credit protections) you might need for the future. For instance, one common offer people receive is protection of credit-card accounts with credit insurance. Under normal circumstances I advise people to decline those offers from credit-card companies. However, there are a few scenarios in which such insurance might make sense. Here's one. Let's say that your company starts firing employees and you've been notified that within 60 days you'll be getting a pink slip and no compensation package. Let's also assume that your becoming a victim of downsizing couldn't have come at a worse time because your spouse took ill and can't work. Under this circumstance, since you have some advance notice, it may well be worth your money to get credit-card insurance protection that allows you to forego or reduce your card payments in the event of a job loss. In this way, even if your money gets tight, you protect your credit standing.

Part of proper credit management involves planning for the unexpected and giving yourself some wiggle room when necessary. That's why it's good to know about your financial options and occasionally to explore competing products and services.

Keeping Abreast of the Ever-Changing World of Credit and Credit Scoring

For people who are fanatical about credit and their scores, and I'll admit I'm among them, one of the ways we maintain a high credit rating is by keeping abreast of new developments in the ever-changing world of credit. For example, in 2009 alone here are some of the major developments that took place:

⇨ In February, consumers stopped being able to get Experian-based FICO® credit scores. Only two FICO® scores are now available, those based on your Equifax and TransUnion reports.

⇨ In May, President Obama signed into law the Credit Card Accountability, Responsibility, and Disclosure Act, also known as the Credit CARD Reform Act, to be rolled out over 15 months.

⇨ In August, two provisions of the Credit CARD Reform Act became effective. One required banks to give consumers 45-days notice before an interest-rate hike, up from the previous requirement of 15 days. Another provision required banks to mail credit-card statements 21 days before the due date, instead of 14 days, in order to give consumers more time to pay their bills.

⇨ In November, Fair Isaac disclosed for the first time the exact range of points your credit score may fall if you make various credit mistakes such as having a late payment or filing for bankruptcy.

You may be asking yourself, "What about me? How can I best stay in the know about all these developments?" One sure-fire way is to read financial and money-oriented publications. Many of these topics also are covered on personal-finance websites. Another strategy is take advantage of the FAQ sections of the three major credit bureaus' and FICO®'s websites. In addition, you can sign up for any free online consumer-advice newsletters and articles posted by Credit.com, CreditKarma.com, and Quizzle.com.

"Ten years ago consumers didn't even know what a credit score was for the most part," says CreditKarma.com CEO Kenneth Lin. "Today most people know what scores are, but I think there's still a lot of ambiguity and confusion about how they work." That's where a company like CreditKarma.com comes into play. In addition to loads of credit-education articles, it offers comparison tools to let you know how your credit stacks up against that of other people in your age group or your state. The firm's "Credit Simulator" helps you to see the cause-and-effect relation between certain actions and your credit score. And then there's its popular Q&A section that lets users submit a question about their personal credit challenges or issues they don't understand. Launched in early 2008, CreditKarma.com now has more than 1 million registered users and has given away several million free credit scores. According to Lin, "We have a very strong focus on credit education and transparency, which I think is lacking in the industry."

Lastly, to keep abreast of credit issues, stay plugged in to what your fellow consumers are saying about credit topics on discussion boards and in chat rooms or through social-networking sites. Some important issue may impact a stranger before it affects you, but that person's online opinions, rants, complaints, or insights could serve as an effective warning for you.

Know the Credit Laws Governing You and Your Creditors

One advantage of knowing the law is that you get to assert your rights under it. Those consumers who are ignorant of the law often get taken advantage of by creditors, bill collectors, and others. Don't let that happen to you. Here are a few quick facts you should know about the rights you have under the Fair Credit Reporting Act (FCRA).

⇨ **You can dispute inaccurate information contained in your file**
Once you tell a consumer-reporting agency that something in your file is wrong, that agency must investigate the item in dispute, typically within 30 days. Ultimately the credit agency must give you a written report summarizing the investigation. It must also provide you with

an updated copy of your credit report if their investigation results in changes to it.

⇨ **Erroneous information must be corrected or deleted from your credit files**
If something is correct, however, that data doesn't have to be removed unless it is outdated or can't be verified.

⇨ **Only businesses with legitimate purposes can view your credit report and only then with your permission**
For instance, in considering your application to them, a creditor, employer, landlord, or insurer can obtain information about you from a credit bureau.

Understanding the Fair Debt Collection Practices Act

Millions of Americans are behind in paying their bills, especially with so many people out of work, but being late on your financial obligations doesn't give debt collectors the right to harass you whenever they want. Under the Fair Debt Collection Practices Act, debt collectors cannot do the following:

⇨ Contact you before 8:00 a.m. or after 9:00 p.m. local time unless you give them permission or unless they have a court order to do so.

⇨ Call you at your job if you tell them that your employer prohibits such calls.

⇨ Contact you if you tell them that you have a lawyer representing you.

To stop a debt collector from harassing you, write them a cease-and-desist letter telling them to end all further contact with you. The first sentence of your letter should say, "I am unable to pay this bill because" or "I refuse to pay this debt because" and then explain your reason. You also have the option of not giving any reason at all. The second sentence should state, "I hereby assert my right under Section 805-C of the Fair

Debt Collection Practices Act to request that you cease any further communication with me." Send this letter via certified mail with a return receipt requested. After the debt collectors receive your letter, they cannot contact you except to indicate that the collection process against you has stopped or that legal action against you is moving forward. Refer to Chapter 10 for more advice on dealing with debt collectors.

The Credit CARD Reform Act Ushers in Big Changes in 2010 and Beyond

Effective in February 2010, a host of changes to your credit-card agreements take effect. For example, the Credit CARD Reform Act does the following:

✳ bans retroactive interest-rate increases (unless you're 60 days or more late in paying your credit-card bill);

✳ restricts default rates to six months if customers pay on time (meaning that, even if your credit-card company charges you a higher rate due to a late payment, it can only do so for six months);

✳ outlaws universal default (refers to the practice of banks' raising your interest rate on one card because you've been late in making a payment on a different card);

✳ mandates that payments be first applied to the highest-rate balances (helps you to pay the least amount of finance charges, cutting your overall borrowing cost);

✳ requires anyone under 21 to have a co-signer to get a credit card;

✳ forbids credit cards from being issued to people under 18;
✳ sets rules for how quickly banks must apply payments;

✳ prohibits fees on payments made via phone and the Internet;

✳ puts a five-year lifespan on gift cards and eliminate their hidden fees;

* requires better disclosure of payment-due dates and late-payment penalties; and

* prevents issuers from establishing early-morning payment deadlines (no due dates before 5:00 p.m. on any business day).

Here's my take on the new law. The downsides, or *potential* risks, to consumers include:

⇨ limited or no grace periods;

⇨ more credit cards with annual fees;

⇨ stricter credit practices (harder to qualify for cards, higher rates, slashed credit lines, or outright closing of accounts);

⇨ creative fees or questionable new practices by banks; and

⇨ more junk mail (banks will try to make up for lost profits by attracting certain new customers).

Overall, however, I think that credit-card reform is a huge win for consumers. I don't buy the banking industry's contention that it will be unjustifiably hurt by the changes. Sure, they'll have diminished profits, but that's after having reaped many billions of dollars in profits based on questionable fees and unfair practices. Nor do I accept the industry's claims that "low income" people will suffer the most because of reduced access to credit. Only time will tell, but my best guess is that banks will tighten up the rules, as they've been doing lately, and hit customers with more fees in the short term.

In the long run, probably, banks will become more competitive with one another and drop those fees and/or overly restrictive terms. When one bank stops imposing annual fees or quits nickel-and-diming card customers, the rest of the industry will take notice and try to do the same.

Lastly, it's important to note that banks still exert a lot of power. For example, they can close your account any time they want, without notice and for any reason. They also can lower your credit line without advance notice, providing they don't impose any fees or hike your interest rate. So credit-card reform is essentially a way to create a more level playing field and bring more fairness into credit-card lending/marketing practices. On the heels of sweeping credit-card changes Congress in 2010 began considering a massive reform of the entire financial services industry. The new regulations are expected to do everything from overhaul mortgage lending to create a national Office of Financial Literacy to protect consumers

In summary, no matter what the laws are today concerning credit and debt issues that impact your rating, recognize that those laws could just as easily change tomorrow. To become a credit-savvy consumer, you must be willing to take the time to educate yourself about credit and scoring matters. No one will do it for you, but that's okay because in the process you'll become financially empowered, recognize a true deal when you see one, steer clear of bogus credit offers, and achieve what once might have seemed totally elusive—Perfect Credit.

Appendices

Appendix A: Credit Bureaus

Equifax
http://www.Equifax.com
Post Office Box 740241
Atlanta, GA 30374
800-685-1111

Experian
http://www.Experian.com
Post Office Box 9556
Allen, TX 75013
877-397-3742

TransUnion
http://www.TransUnion.com
2 Baldwin Place
Post Office Box 2000
Chester, PA 19022
800-888-4213

Innovis
http://www.Innovis.com
Post Office Box 1358
Columbus, Ohio 43216-1358
800-540-2505

Appendix B: Sample Dispute Letter to Credit Bureaus

Date
(Sent certified mail with a return receipt requested)

Your Name
Your Address
Your City, State, Zip Code

(_____) Insert name of bureau: Equifax, Experian, or TransUnion
Address
City, State, Zip Code

To Whom It May Concern:

This letter is to request that you investigate inaccurate information contained in my (_____) credit file. (Fill in the blank with Equifax, Experian, or TransUnion, depending on the credit bureau to which you are writing.) The information I am disputing pertains to the (_____) of the account listed below: (Fill in the blank with the word "ownership" or "status," depending on the type of dispute.)

(_____) Account, with the account number ending as (_____) (Put the account name and the last four digits of the account in the respective blanks.)

The data reported about me is erroneous because (_____). (Insert your own reason or fill in the blank, as appropriate, with one of the following reasons: "This is not my account"; "I have never paid late"; "I paid this account in full"; "This account was included in my bankruptcy"; "The balance shown is incorrect"; or "This account was opened fraudulently, and I am the victim of identity theft.")

Indicated below are my full name, date of birth, Social Security number, and address for the past two years:

Full Name: _____

Date of Birth: _____

Social Security Number: _____

Address, City, State, Zip Code: _____

Also enclosed is a copy of (_____) (Insert "my driver's license," "a recent utility bill," or "a recent credit-card statement.") so that you can verify my address and identity. Please investigate this matter promptly and delete the incorrect information as required by law.

Sincerely,

Your Signature
Your Name

Enclosures (List what you are enclosing. Only send copies, not originals. Also mention whether you are providing any supporting documents to prove your claim. By law this information must be forwarded by the credit bureau to the creditor, bill collector, or furnisher of the erroneous information.)

Appendix C: Holiday Credit Quiz

If you had to classify your credit report as a holiday, which one would it be?

Martin Luther King, Jr. Day: Your credit report makes you want to repeat Dr. King's mantra, "We shall overcome. We shall overcome. We shall overcome some day."

Valentine's Day: You've managed debt and credit so wisely that people might be tempted to think you have a love affair with your bankers/creditors.

April Fool's Day: Your credit report contains so many mistakes and so much outdated information that somebody *must* be playing a trick on you.

Cinco De Mayo: Your credit report might as well be in Spanish—or Greek, Italian, Russian, Japanese, or any other language you don't speak—because you can't really understand most of what's in there.

Flag Day: Your credit report just makes you want to raise a flag, a white one, and surrender.

Halloween: Your credit report is downright frightening.

Thanksgiving: You are thankful and relieved that your credit report looks pretty good.

Even though several of these holidays might be applicable, pick the one that best sums up how you feel about your most recent credit report. Haven't taken a peek at your report lately? Then you haven't been paying attention! Get those reports now and then come back to take this quick quiz.

No matter what the state of your credit, even if you immediately see negative information in your files, you needn't go off the deep end. Calm yourself down when you delve into your report by remembering that your credit file is a bit like Christmas: there's got to be some good cheer (hey, you do have a credit rating after all); a bit of good will (somebody extended you credit once upon a time); and maybe even a present or two (regardless of whether you've been naughty or nice). What are the biggest presents of all from reviewing your credit report? It's the twofold gift of education and self-empowerment in learning how to manage credit and debt wisely.

Don't forget to write me at info@themoneycoach.net and let me know your response to this quiz. Please put the words "Holiday Credit Quiz" in the subject line of your email.

Appendix D: Consumer Resources

Online Resources:

http://www.AnnualCreditReport.com
http://www.CardRatings.com
http://www.CreditCards.com
http://www.Credit.com
http://www.CreditKarma.com
http://www.FreeCreditReport.com
http://www.ftc.gov
http://www.Quizzle.com
http://www.VantageScore.com
http://www.Zendough.com

Books:

Credit Scores and Credit Reports: How the System Really Works, by Evan Hendricks

How You Can Profit from Credit Cards: Using Credit to Improve Your Financial Life and Bottom Line, by Curtis Arnold

You're Nothing But a Number: Why Achieving Great Credit Scores Should Be on Your List of Wealth-Building Strategies, by John Ulzheimer

Your Credit Score: How to Fix, Improve, and Protect the Three-Digit Number That Shapes Your Financial Future, by Liz Pulliam Weston

Zero Debt: The Ultimate Guide to Financial Freedom, by Lynnette Khalfani-Cox

Zero Debt for College Grads: From Student Loans to Financial Freedom, by Lynnette Khalfani-Cox

INDEX

Made in the USA
Lexington, KY
12 December 2010